PROJECT
MANAGEMENT
DISASTERS
& how to survive them

'Events, dear boy, events.'

Harold Macmillan

PROJECT MANAGEMENT
MANAGEMENT
DISASTERS
& how to survive them

DAVID NICKSON with **SUZY SIDDONS**

KOGAN
PAGE

London and Philadelphia

For my beloved wife, editorial adviser, collaborator and
all-round good egg, Suzy Siddons.

Publisher's note
Every possible effort has been made to ensure that the information contained in this book is accurate at the time of going to press, and the publishers and authors cannot accept responsibility for any errors or omissions, however caused. No responsibility for loss or damage occasioned to any person acting, or refraining from action, as a result of the material in this publication can be accepted by the editor, the publisher or any of the authors.

First published in Great Britain and the United States in 2005 by Kogan Page Limited
This edition 2006

120 Pentonville Road
London N1 9JN
United Kingdom
www.kogan-page.co.uk

525 South 4th Street, #241
Philadelphia PA 19147
USA

© David Nickson, 2005, 2006

The right of David Nickson to be identified as the author of this work has been asserted by him in accordance with the Copyright, Designs and Patents Act 1988.

ISBN 0 7494 4780 X

British Library Cataloguing-in-Publication Data

A CIP record for this book is available from the British Library.

Library of Congress Cataloging-in-Publication Data

Nickson, David.
    Project management disasters and how to survive them / David Nickson with Suzy Siddons.
      p. cm.
    Rev ed. of: Project disasters & how to survive them. 2005.
    Includes bibliographical references and index.
    ISBN 0-7494-4780-X
    1. Emergency management. 2. Project management. 3. Risk management. 4. Strategic planning.
I. Siddons, Suzy II. Nickson, David, Project disasters & how to survive them. III. Title.
    HD49.N53 2006
    658.4′04—dc22

                                    2006013219

Typeset by JS Typesetting Ltd, Porthcawl, Mid Glamorgan
Printed and bound in the United States by Thomson-Shore, Inc

Contents

Foreword

Every project manager at some time in his or her career will have a project that for some reason fails to deliver its intended outcome in terms of time, costs and/or quality. Sometimes it is clearly evident why the project has failed; however, this is little comfort to the client organization or the project managers, who are more than likely to be remembered for their failures rather than their successes. On occasions, the reason for failure is a mystery, as things seem to be going well until something comes from 'out of the blue'. And that is generally part of the problem, isn't it? We just don't know what we don't know, and even after carrying out the most extensive of risk assessments prior to the commencement of the project it is those 'out of the blue' things that hold a lot of responsibility for project failures. Is that truly it – we can't control these things? Surely not! OK, in some cases, projects are scuppered owing to unforeseen events, but in many others the failure is due to poor management, poor communication or lack of project definition as identified by David in this wonderful insight into project failures. So what happens once disaster hits? Is it a case of let it happen or do something about it?

David's examples show a wide variety of events that may have been recovered through the application of these principles. The book is not before time either, with the UK's Office of Government Commerce highlighting the need to have more independence in reviewing its projects by the recent introduction of the Gateway Review Process, whereby Government projects are reviewed by independent review teams at predetermined points during the project, thus avoiding some of the embarrassing projects that the Government has managed or failed to manage in the past. It's high time the lessons learned from previous project failures are shared with others in order that these lessons can be applied to help recover 'project near misses'.

I thoroughly enjoyed this book as it reminded me of similar situations that I have seen during my years in a Government procurement office – not only to reminisce, but to highlight how easy it might have been to turn potential disasters into successes.

I have worked with David and his wife Suzy for many years and they have demonstrated, many times, that they are a management force to be reckoned with and that two heads are certainly better than one!

Peter Ritson

Peter Ritson has worked in logistics and procurement for more than 25 years. The majority of these have been in Government organizations.

Preface

The original idea for this book was to address an obvious gap in the project management market. There are hundreds, probably thousands, of books telling you how to manage projects, risk, teams and budgets. However, few, if any, of these deal with what happens when a project becomes a real disaster. The author's theory is that this is because all such books are based upon a method, approach, set of tools or what-have-you that will prevent any such disasters taking place. Indeed, the author's own book on project management (*Managing Projects*) would fit nicely into this category. The nearest such books get to disaster management is to look at risks and related risk plans. Initial research supported this theory; take the following extract from *PRINCE 2: An Outline*: 'In broadest terms, a project is a managed collection of activities to bring about a desired change. PRINCE 2 provides a framework whereby a bridge between a current state of affairs and a planned future state may be constructed.' It goes on to say that 'PRINCE 2 focuses attention on products rather than activities, ensuring that the organization gets what it wants, providing more reliable estimates etc etc.' The implication is that by following the methodology, you will get a result. To be fair, it does say that you need to look at risks, business cases and all the rest and review them as time passes. It is a good methodology and one well worth using. Other methodologies are sold in a similar way: follow the recipe, obey the rules, and all will be well. The implication is that the world may not be your oyster, but it can at least be your ham sandwich. The last thing you want to do is to suggest that you can follow the process, do things right, and still have a disaster.

So, there seemed to be a good logical reason why there are few books on project disasters (only two have been included in the bibliography, because they were all the author could find, and one of them was out of print). There are, of course, numerous books on disasters in general, many written for the delight of the prurient. But, having sold the concept of this book to Kogan Page and having got started on the research, it quickly became apparent that there might be another reason for a dearth of titles covering project disasters. Once you ask to talk to someone about their involvement in a project that has gone wrong, they become unaccountably shy. For example, a request for information was placed on the website of the British Computer Society's Project Management Special Interest Group. This elicited not a single attributable response, despite being there for several months and apparently being mentioned in a newsletter. Fortunately, there are so many IT-related disasters that this reticence did not reduce the overall contribution from this market sector. Also an army of PR, marketing and press officers leap forward wielding metaphorical batons, water cannon and CS gas sprays to fend off even the most friendly and positive enquiry. In fact, the usual response for a request for an interview is to ignore you and hope you go away. Nobody wants to be associated with a disaster, even when the outcome was a good one. Fortunately, it was possible to obtain a substantial body of 'off the record' comments and to mine the rich vein of press coverage on disasters. The army of the press core counters the PR marketing and press office battalions. There are also those who believe, with some credibility, that problems stem from taking command-and-control methodologies rather than an organic approach to deciding what needs to be done and having those with the knowledge decide on the approach.

Should it come to writing a sequel to this book, the author sincerely hopes that the positive, non-blaming, approach presented here will make people more accessible, but he is not holding his breath. In the meantime, this book aims to help those experiencing a disaster first hand and how to survive it.

Acknowledgements

The author thanks all the people who have helped, or were happy to be quoted, in preparing this book. Others are thanked who provided off-the-record interviews and information; you know who you are! In addition, sources of information such as the trade and national press, the BBC, ITN, books and libraries were investigated and reviewed; as far as possible, these are also included in the bibliography, but the author apologizes for any that got missed in the compilation.

The following individuals are thanked for their time and support: Ian Birch, Jan Carter, Chris Cox, Professor Jim McDermid, Pauline Goodwin, Ailsa Marks, Peter Ritson, John Seddon, Suzy Siddons and, finally, the anonymous reviewer employed by Kogan Page to look at the first complete draft and Angela Bailey, the copy-editor.

DISCLAIMER

Because of the understandable reluctance of individuals and organizations to be identified with project disasters, many case studies have been disguised and some have been merged. For example, an organization might be referred to as Company C; readers are encouraged not to jump to conclusions as to the identities of these organizations. Also, because some of the information had to be obtained second, and sometimes third hand, or via other sources of reference, it is possible that errors in the detail of specific disasters may exist. Furthermore, some technical accounts have been simplified for a more general audience. It should be kept in mind that the key point is to illustrate how disasters come about and how to survive them; the examples are not meant to be treated as academically rigorous. That said, where individuals and organizations have been directly quoted, every effort has been made to ensure the accuracy of the information presented, and any errors that have crept through are accidental.

Introduction

This book has been written to address a gap in the project, risk, business, and human resources management market relating to projects that go very badly wrong. Accepting that projects can go horribly wrong and recognizing that this is something that can be dealt with is the main aim of the work. The intention is to be realistic; the reader should be under no illusion that there is a magic wand to wave that will turn a fiasco into a triumph. However, a more positive outcome is possible if the right measures are taken. This is a survival skills handbook from project workers.

There are many famous project disasters that can serve as examples, some good and some bad. The *Apollo 13* moon shot is one of the best; here was a real disaster that had a positive outcome, and it will feature prominently in this book. A malfunction on the outbound trip caused major damage to the spacecraft. NASA's mission-control specialists, support staff and managers were able to work with the remote team on board to develop a solution which got them back home safely to Earth. Although this is a very high-profile, high-risk and high-stakes example, it still makes an excellent case study of what can be done when something goes very wrong with a project. Lessons can be learnt from this that are useful when applied in a more 'down-to-earth' business project environment. The book will draw on famous, not so famous, and totally obscure project disasters to illustrate what can be done when things get out of hand.

The examples and case studies presented in this book are all real, though some have been blended together to illustrate particular points and others have had changes made to protect the identities of those involved. A recurrent theme throughout the research was an unwillingness to 'go on the record', so there are more anonymous examples than the author and the publisher's marketing department would have wished. They come from a variety of industries and organizations, though it must be confessed that the IT industry seems to account for a disproportionate percentage of project disasters. This is not just because the author has some background in IT but also because this seems to reflect reality. However, examples have also been drawn from engineering, aviation and space technology, and the financial and service industries. Although the causes of these presented disasters will be investigated, a major theme of the book will be to look at what those involved did after the event and how effective their actions were in improving the outcome. In some cases, it will be clear that more could have been done; in other cases, it will be seen that there was little else to do but accept the inevitable. Even then, a disaster does not mean the abandonment of hope.

Note: In this book, the use of the term 'case study' is intended to represent a more 'worked' scenario than an example that is more one dimensional and shorter. However, no great attempt has been made to achieve consistency with this nomenclature – this is not a textbook for a formal methodology.

Disaster means different things to different people; one person's hiccup is another's catastrophe. In this book, the definition of a project disaster is based upon not being able to meet the major goals of the project to time/budget. This can be a looser definition than might be thought, as many projects are disasters because their goals were not defined in the first place. Entire teams have been known to spend years working towards, well, nothing very specific actually. Some projects are completed, seemingly success-fully, but are found after the event to be completely irrelevant to the business needs of the organization. For that reason, some disasters can even go undetected. Chapter 1 will expand the nature of this definition further.

This book has been written to help anyone, and everyone, who finds themselves in the middle of a project disaster. The sugges-tions made are given to help people make the best of the situation and increase the probability of a positive end result. A core value of this book is avoiding the blame game, and the emphasis is on triumphing over adversity – a 'can do' approach to trouble. It should be read by project managers, business managers, HR, PR and marketing staff, and anyone else who thinks the project they are involved with is a disaster.

Having said whom it is for and what it is for, it is also important to make clear what the book is not intended to do. This is not a book on self-help; it is not a book about psychological and trauma counselling. The disasters here are on a project, or possibly program, scale. Dealing with natural disasters such as earth-quakes and tidal waves, air crashes, acts of terrorism and the like are not covered here, and neither are the support services that go with such events within the scope. Although HR and PR issues are covered, these are dealt with only in so far as they can help with surviving a project disaster, not the implications for career progression, job security, public liability or personal sanity. Finally, this is not an academic treatise; research has been done, references and acknowledgements made, but academic rigour and review have not been thoroughly applied to this work. The author has blended his own experiences with those of others and has adopted a more journalistic approach in the hope of produc-ing something readable and helpful. No guarantees of efficacy are offered.

SAMPLE CASE STUDY

Although examples will be taken from high-profile and high-risk disasters, the type of project disaster that the book is aimed to help with is illustrated in the following short case study.

Project overview	This was a project that had the goal of upgrading the IT desktop equipment for an internal, but customer-facing department. The reason for the project was to bring the administrative staff in line with the corporate IT platform, get them all onto the internal e-mail system and provide them with effective access to internet/intranet systems. Once this was done, they would have better tools that would make it easier, and quicker to perform their roles. The clients would then benefit from improved response times to queries, and the staff would not feel that they were, 'at the bottom of the pile' when it came to equipment/facilities. The latter was a significant factor as it was leading to higher staff turnover than was desirable. This was starting to have a negative effect on customer perceptions.
Disaster	The overseas parent organization withdrew budgetary approval for the project after it was announced and part of the roll-out had taken place. The company was having local financial difficulties so decided to claw back money from its subsidiaries. This was to be a short-term 'hiccup' but the budget would not be fully reinstated for at least six months.
Situation	Of the new equipment, 25 per cent had been delivered; this was a phased roll-out and the equipment was being ordered and delivered in batches. The second batch of 25 per cent was ordered, but the remaining equipment had not yet been committed to. This meant that there would be a 50 per cent shortfall. The project team was made up of in-

	house staff seconded from their usual operations work; they still had 'day job' responsibilities.
Impact	Because this was an internal project, it benefited from not directly affecting external customers. However, it could easily have been seen as a career reversal for those involved. It also had the potential to seriously demotivate staff who were directly in contact with the organization's customers. It also meant that these people were not really fully equipped to do their jobs.
Action taken	Fortunately, because the project team was in-house, it was possible to keep the team together for a short time, even though the overall funding had been withdrawn. This meant that the option existed to make the best of a poor situation. As disasters go, this was mild one. The existing project plan was put on hold and options were considered at a brain-storming session that was held off-site. HR and line management were included in this meeting so that all those required to implement any next steps were present and had obtained authority to make decisions. Option one was to abandon the project and put the new equipment in store for spare use and new issue across the whole organization. This was the simplest option and had the advantage of simplicity and modest cost (of capital tied up in what would be about 12 months of stock holding in equipment). It had major 'soft' disadvantages associated with going back on promises to the administrative staff, leaving them all with equipment that was not really up to the job needed and leaving the project team feeling that they had wasted their time to date. The department already had high staff turnover, and lack of continuity was adversely impacting customers. At a slightly higher cost, it was seen that the initial 25 per cent batch of equipment could be deployed by the project team, operating in conjunction with the IT department more or less as per the original plan. However, it would not be possible

	to keep the whole team together long enough to do this for the next 25 per cent. It was decided to try a 'self-help' approach for this second tranche of equipment. The first 25 per cent would be split evenly among the administrators, some of whom (selected on experience grounds) would be given some additional training in installing the equipment (this was simply a case of unpacking it, connecting it together and connecting it to power and communications sockets). They would then call the IT department who would remotely configure the equipment. This would cause some disruption and additional work for the support desk but meant that 50 per cent of the administrators would get the new equipment and facilities. These were chosen on their experience and workload. So, a new project was set up to prioritize where the new equipment would be both most effective, and most fairly located. HR would undertake a communications exercise to ensure that the administrative staff was aware what was happening and how they were being given the best solution possible under the new circumstances.
Outcome	Maximum use of the available equipment was made. This was done in such a way that the staff appreciated that it was done as fairly as possible rather than merely as expediently as possible. The communications exercise, which cost very little, meant that this approach was well understood and appreciated. Consequently, staff accepted that they had been considered and that their needs were part of the solution. The project was not simply abandoned, and some of the goals were achieved with a clear view of how the project would be completed when trading conditions permitted. In addition, the project team felt that they had achieved something useful, and their morale ended on a high.

STRUCTURE

The paragraphs below show the chapters and what they cover; each chapter has been written so that it works on its own. It is perfectly practical to dip in and out of this book in search of information, and to sort and find it without having to resort to cross-referencing. A primary goal has been to make the book easy to use and easy to read, and for the benefits to be quickly realized.

The *Introduction* provides an overview of the book, its scope, who it is (and is not) for, how to use it and a brief description of the contents of each chapter and the appendices.

Chapter 1: Definition and scope explains that not everything that seems like a disaster is one. What makes a project a disaster is defined here, and examples are presented of real project disasters, some famous, along with some of the consequences. The scope of the disasters and the extent of related activities are further defined here.

Chapter 2: Why project disasters happen examines the causes of project disasters. Understanding why a project has become a disaster is the first step towards rectifying the problem, if that is going to be possible. Several 'classic' examples of disaster are covered, and they serve as templates for comparison with the reader's own disaster. As with novels where there are only a limited number of actual plots available, there are also only a limited number of fundamental causes of project disasters. Recognizing this fact makes this first step that much easier. A theme of this chapter will be that there is seldom a single cause of a disaster and that the causes often interact or form part of a chain of events.

Chapter 3: Learning from disasters demonstrates that there is much that can be learnt from disasters that have befallen others. Examples of disasters are presented, and the strategies adopted by those involved are examined with a view to seeing what did, or did not, work. The emphasis will be on how to learn from the disasters without descending into the blame game. It will be seen that what works in one case does not always work in another, and taking recovery action by rote is not a safe solution when in the middle of a disaster.

Chapter 4: Risk and reality concentrates on identifying threats to a project, assessing them and identifying containment and contingency actions to deal with them. Reality limits the extent to which this can be applied to any project, and this chapter looks at risk management and why disasters still happen. Why this is not a failure of risk management, but rather is a consequence of the pragmatism that has to be adopted if any project is to be allowed to start in the first place is examined. The perils of paying lip service and/or watering down risk management are identified.

Chapter 5: Human resources considers what HR can, and should, do to help staff through a project disaster. The emphasis is on practical, rather than personal, support, although the importance of identifying when personal support is required is not ignored. The ways in which HR can mitigate the impact of any 'blame-game' culture that may exist are discussed, together with examples of where HR have made things better, and also of where they have made things worse. Skills that those involved with disasters might need are evaluated. and the ways in which these skills are related to training are identified. It is explained how the retention and redeployment of staff should be considered in a positive way

Chapter 6: Public relations points out that, in many organizations, PR (and maybe marketing) will need to be, and indeed may insist on being, involved in anything that counts as a disaster so that the outside world is presented with the right image. Examples where this has worked, and also where it has backfired, are given. The benefits of an honest approach are provided together with the pitfalls that await those who choose to misrepresent a disaster in an attempt to disguise it.

Chapter 7: Disaster and the organization explores the interactions between the project and the wider world, specifically with the organization within which the project exists. The ways in which the failing project impacts the organization and the ways in which the organization impacts the project are both explored in this chapter. Topics such as financial and morale issues, together with lost opportunities, resource and image implications are covered. In addition, the culture attributes of organizations which are more, or less, likely to produce a positive outcome are considered. The effect of the 'blame culture' is given particular attention.

Chapter 8: Triumph over adversity examines how best to support and lead project teams through disasters, how to reward efforts to keep going, and management strategies for coping. In every disaster, there exists an opportunity. The objective here is to look at examples where people spotted opportunities and capitalized on them. These may be spin-off benefits, or solutions to problems that were not even identified before things went wrong. Looking outside of the immediate issues can be made possible by disasters and can potentially lead to better times. Techniques needed by management and team members alike are considered, for example, brainstorming, SWOT analysis and so forth.

Chapter 9: Recipes and survival skills presents a summary of a disaster-recovery recipe, together with the survival strategies that might be implemented and a description of the benefits that can be expected. Checklists of points to consider when a disaster occurs – including a diagnostic method for identifying what to consider next – are suggested. It may be unpleasant for those involved, but a disaster is not always a failure and can be turned into something positive. It may not be possible to recover from the current problem, but at least lessons can be learnt that can be applied another time. Key skills are also considered, for example how to give bad news without causing total despair.

Chapter 10: What not to do provides guidance, based on research advice, as to what not to do and gives concrete examples of actions that have been shown not to help the situation. This chapter can be used as a quick check to make sure that the wrong actions are not being taken. For those under severe pressure of time, this chapter can be read in minutes.

Appendix 1: Teams describes specific problems experienced within teams and how to cope with them, for example setting objectives, dealing with Group Think, and the team environment.

Appendix 2: Stress identifies stress and its likely impact, together with strategies for helping to reduce it.

Note to readers: In this book, cross references are simply to other chapters rather than to specific entries. The intention is to encourage browsing. Those who do not wish to browse are recommended to make use of the index. No apology is made for this serendipity friendly, but un-textbook like approach.

NOTE ON SOURCES

When researching this book, the author and his main collaborator, his wife, used all the traditional methods of interviews, journal and periodical searches, reviewing reference material, their own and their friends' experiences and so forth. In many cases, sources wished not to be identified, but in other cases it became clear that there were common patterns emerging. Consequently, the presentation of the research described in this book has taken various forms: scenarios; case studies; examples and quotations. Scenarios have typically been made up of a blend of sources that serve to protect sources and also allows specific points to be highlighted more clearly than is often the case in a single real sample. Most of the case studies are real, though some have been simplified for clarity and brevity. In some cases the definition of a project has been stretched slightly – a space shot has a beginning and an end and so has been considered as a project, some may disagree with this. The examples and quotations given are as accurate as possible and are attributed where appropriate. However, in many cases, it was hard to get people to admit to having anything to do with a disaster, or else they denied that it was a disaster at all; that in itself is something to learn about project disasters. Indeed, when asked by Kogan Page to provide some more European attributable examples, one from the publishing industry was offered but it was turned down. People are even sensitive to mentions of disasters in their own industry.

As a case in point, a famous scientist was approached after a somewhat spectacular and newsworthy failed experiment. His reaction was that 'there has been no disaster' and that he did not 'give interviews to authors writing books'. Although not possible in this example, getting around attitudes such as this requires a degree of diplomacy and determination at least as great as required by a project manager actually experiencing a disaster.

HEALTH CHECK

This book is firmly grounded in reality; when reading an early draft of part of this book, my wife and collaborator, pointed out that it seemed to give the impression that all disasters can have a good outcome. This is obviously not the case; the fact that something has reached the stage of being described as a disaster means that the overall outcome is usually poor. The key words here are, **'and how to survive them'**; the emphasis is on getting the best possible result – not working miracles.

SUMMARY

There are two positive outcomes that it is hoped that this book will achieve. The first is that by studying the causes of disasters and, at their first sign, adopting good recovery strategies, there will be fewer disasters overall. The second is that by avoiding a blame culture, and instead adopting a combination of 'can do' and lateral thinking, the best route to survival for those involved in a disaster will be identified. There is also a third, hidden, outcome that the author hopes for; that people will become more open about disasters so that it will become easier to learn from them and therefore to avoid them.

TERMS AND ABBREVIATIONS

In order to avoid repetition, a number of terms have been used in this book without supporting explanations in the adjacent text necessarily being included. The following list presents these terms, together with a brief explanation as a starting point for finding further information.

APM	Association of Project Managers – professional body and source of expertise/standards.
Back office	A function where processes take place to support client-related business activities, e.g. matching invoices to customer orders.
BCS	British Computer Society.
Broadsheet	An up-market newspaper with in-depth coverage.
Critical path	The activities that define the time it will take for a project to complete; any delay to a critical-path activity will delay (or stop) the whole project.
DABGA	Denial, anger, bargaining, grief, acceptance. The stages people go through when presented with a profound change or problem.
GANTT	A bar chart showing project activities against time (Henri Gantt).
HR	Human resources, also known as personnel.
HRM	Human resources management.
ISEB	Information Systems Examinations Board (of the BCS).
IT	Information technology.
KISS	Keep it simple sir (or whatever term you wish to adopt).
NASA	National Aeronautics and Space Administration – US space agency.
OGC	Office of Government Commerce (UK Government).
PERT	Project evaluation and review technique (originally developed for the manufacture of nuclear submarines).

PM	Project manager.
PMI	Project Management Institute – professional body and source of expertise/standards.
PR	Public relations.
PRINCE	Projects in a controlled environment.
Quality plan	A set of documents describing how quality will be maintained for a project.
RAEng	Royal Academy of Engineering.
Red top	Tabloid or populist newspaper.
Risk plan	A set of documents describing risks to a project and related mitigation and contingency plans.
SHF	Super high frequency.
SMART	Simple, measurable, achievable, realistic, time frame. Test for achievable goals.
SME	Small to medium enterprise – a middle-sized business as opposed to a multinational corporation.
STOP	Share the question; think about how you're going to answer it; only answer the question; politely check that your answer is OK. A useful tool in question handling.
SWOT	Strength, weakness, opportunity, threat.
TV	Television.
WBS	Work breakdown structure – a hierarchical analysis of a project and its activities.
WIMP	Windows, imaging, mouse pointer – graphical interface computing.

1

Definition and scope

Before going much further, it is important to define what is meant by a disaster, as far as this book is concerned. The following extract from the author's 1974 edition of *Webster's Dictionary* defines disaster as '1 obs: an unfavourable aspect of a planet or star; 2 : a sudden calamitous event bringing great damage, loss or destruction; *broadly* a sudden or great misfortune'. The first of these is largely academic as it shows the Latin roots of the word (*dis – and astro – star*); astrology is not within the remit of this book. The second is the relevant one. The same dictionary includes the definition of a project as 'a planned undertaking'. So, a project disaster can therefore be defined as a 'sudden or great misfortune affecting a planned undertaking'.

Note: A disaster may be sudden or great or both, but it does not have to be both; some disasters creep up on projects, others arrive with a bang.

What it means for those involved is usually extreme chaos, uncertainty and fear for the future, if not for their jobs. This is reinforced because the current prevalent culture in most Western businesses, reinforced by lawyers, management gurus and Health and Safety specialists is that 'everything that happens is some-one's fault'. This may, or may not be true, but it isn't helpful. There is an old saying that 'in the aftermath of a failed project, the guilty are promoted and the innocent punished.' So, the first thing that has to be done to help in surviving is to break free of the blame culture in favour of an open and 'can do' one. To help with this, a new definition of a disaster is called for, and this is the one that will be used for the rest of this book. '*A project disaster is when an event has happened that makes it impossible to carry on as before and still achieve the objective.*'

An important fact to keep in mind is that, in most cases, project disasters do not bring the organization to total collapse and rarely bring about the termination of careers. What seems like a disaster at the time can, if approached in the right way, not only be survived but also become a new opportunity to succeed. Of course, this is always easier to appreciate when you are not the one actually involved. That is why one of the survival techniques that has been seen to work is to get someone to provide an outside view.

Perhaps the most famous project disaster in the world hitherto was captured in the following exchange of messages (the times are mission time in hours, minutes and seconds after launch):

55:55:20 – Swigert: 'Okay, Houston, we've had a problem here.'
55:55:28 – Lousma: 'This is Houston. Say again please.'
55:55:35 – Lovell: 'Houston, we've had a problem. We've had a main B bus undervolt.'

This was the point when the folk safely back on Earth at Mission Control learnt about the project disaster on *Apollo 13*. When you are out in space and something has gone very wrong, it is easy to know that your project has a potential disaster on its hands. In the more mundane world of business projects, there is unlikely to be as dramatic a conversation as this that announces the event. However, there will have been clear signs, and these will be considered later in the book. First things first: we need to define what a project is and understand something about why it is different.

It is worth noting that to solve this disaster the *Apollo 13* astronauts called on an 'outside' view from the mission-control specialists back on Earth.

WHAT IS A PROJECT?

Before going too much further, it is worth defining what a project actually is. In 1985, Cleland and Kerzner defined a project as 'A combination of human and non-human resources pulled together in a temporary organization to achieve a specific purpose'.

There are, of course, grey areas. Cars on a production line are produced to a fixed budget by a team of people with a specified end result and a timetable, but it is stretching the concept to call these project teams. However, building a large ocean-going vessel, such as an ocean liner, most certainly can be considered as such; indeed, the project evaluation and estimation tool PERT came out of the nuclear submarine construction programmes of the 1950s. The intention here is not to be shackled by a pedantic definition but to be able to choose examples from a fairly wide constituency in order to illustrate the sorts of problems that occur in the project world.

In the book *Managing Projects*, the author, in conjunction with Suzy Siddons, defined a project as 'a one-off finite piece of work with fixed start and end points and a clear objective. The difference between a project and ongoing work is that a project has a defined beginning and end, as opposed to being part of a continuing activity. For example, building a house is a project, living in one is not.' Figure 1.1 shows how a project relates to the outside world.

Note: Various organizations and professional bodies, such as the UK Government's OGC (Office of Government Commerce), the PMI (Project Management Institute) or APM (Association of Project Managers), have their own definitions of what a project is. For example, the OGC's PRINCE 2 definition is 'a managed collection of activities to bring about a desired change'. For the purposes of this book, this alternative definition would work just

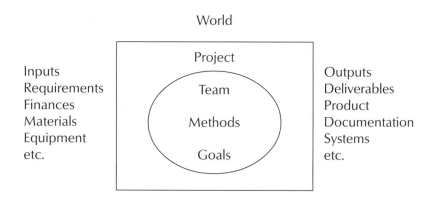

Figure 1.1 Relationship between a project and the outside world

as well – it is left as an exercise for the reader to look up these other definitions and compare and contrast them if they wish – but the definition presented in *Managing Projects* seems as good as any. At the time of writing, *Managing Projects* was on the approved reading list for the British Computer Society's ISEB (Information Systems Examinations Board) project management syllabus. That said, the author acknowledges that the definition of a project has been stretched a little in some of the examples. However, it was considered that the lessons learnt justified the amount of elastic required!

These definitions are all well and good, but it is important to appreciate certain attributes of projects (Figure 1.2).

Note: Holiday travel is a project. Many people don't recognize this, and the fact that they don't plan what they are doing explains all those scenes on television programmes dedicated to budget airlines. There is always an episode where members of the travelling public abuse check-in staff who have closed the gate, and the travellers miss their flight. This is invariably because the holiday-makers haven't allowed for any contingency plans in the event of problems in their journey to the airport. The author considers these check-in staff to practically be saints. The old saying 'failing to plan is planning to fail' applies here.

Feature	Description
Complexity	Projects typically involve a number of separate activities that may have varying degrees of co-dependency. They often require a range of skills and technologies to be harnessed together to achieve the end result. They are usually affected by the environment in which they exist, an environment outside their direct control.
Individual	A project is a one off. Even if it is similar to a previous one, it is still unique. Pilots will tell you that every time they land an aircraft it is different – even when it is the same aircraft at the same airport on the same day of the week for the tenth time; projects are just the same. Bridge-building is another good example – ask any construction project manager who has worked on one and they will tell you that every one is unique. This 'one off' nature is a key property of any project.
Constrained	The budget, timetable, resources, and specifications are all things that are routinely constrained on a project. Even when one is left out, for example when the United States decided to go to the Moon during the Cold War, the budget was not constrained but there was a specific goal and a clear maximum timetable within which to achieve it.
Deliverables	There should be a well-defined set of deliverable items (sometimes called products, which can lead to confusion, as real products are things that are produced time after time, for example cars on a production line). A common cause of disaster is when these deliverables are not closely or completely defined.

Figure 1.2 Project attributes

Project and products

In this book, some of the disasters that are described befell what might be seen as products; however, they were chosen because it was in the supporting projects that the real causes of the problems were found. Products are brought into being by projects – these may be to do with the design of the product, the marketing, or the factory systems for production, but there will inevitably have been a series of projects that were completed before any product comes to the market. At the top end of the scale, aircraft manufacturers have built huge physical and transport infrastructures to set up the production lines for airliners. Both Boeing and Airbus have managed extremely complex and successful projects of this kind.

Projects and programmes

Organizations often draw a distinction between a project and a programme, where a programme is considered to be a set of projects. In many cases, a sort of job-title inflation has crept in. For example, the person who used to be supervisor or team leader often now gets the title of manager. Therefore, many projects are now termed programmes (after all, if you can divide a project into tasks and sub-tasks, then you can just as well call them projects and, bingo, you have a programme!) – project managers then become programme managers. To make life simple in this book, the terms programme and project are used interchangeably, though the preference is for use of the word project. Anyone who has the job title of programme manager, should feel free to read that title for project manager in this book.

SCOPE: WHEN IS A DISASTER NOT A DISASTER?

In this book, the scope of project disasters is limited to those not involving the loss of human life (though some of the examples came close). This is a book about business projects not about natural disasters, the effects of war or other catastrophes.

Some disasters are clear cut – the Mars probe that hit the target rather than orbiting it leaves no room for doubt. However, it is not always the case that something that is called a disaster is one, and it is certainly true that not all disasters are failures.

Example: Scottish Assembly building

The original estimate for the Scottish Assembly building had been variously reported at between £40 million and £50 million at the time of writing, and before the building was completed this had risen to around £400 million. By any standards of budgetary control, this is a disaster. Indeed, when it was first discussed, there was even a lower estimate of £10 million – representing a 4,000 per cent overrun. But is the project a disaster? The parliament building is able to fulfil its function and has met goals relating to a building of status.

Note: After this section of the book was drafted, the final cost of the Scottish Assembly building, reached £431 million, and it was three years late. HM Queen Elizabeth II opened it on Saturday 9 October 2004.

Example: Channel Tunnel

Completed in 1993 and opened in 1994, the Channel Tunnel has never made a profit to date and is widely considered to be a financial disaster. However, it is undoubtedly a major engineering success. It is hoped that within the next 10 years it should start to operate at a profit; perhaps then it will be seen as a complete success.

ACCEPTING THAT A DISASTER HAS HAPPENED

The other side of the coin is when people do not recognize that a disaster has happened. For example, in 2004 a survey (commissioned by Microsoft) of 300 IT and business project managers from UK companies found that 15 per cent of projects were scrapped before completion – but that managers thought that 19 per cent should have been. The gap of 4 per cent was thought to be costing the average large company (with 159 concurrent projects) £13.4 million every year, according to the research, which was presented at an IT directors' forum in May 2004. Many of the people interviewed by the author thought that this was somewhat optimistic; some felt that as many as two-thirds of all projects exceeded budgets/timetables and up to a third of projects 'failed'. What matters here is not the percentage, but the fact that there is a culture of not accepting that a disaster has occurred. This is usually only a short-term factor as real project disasters become increasingly hard to hide. It is also counterproductive as the longer the problem is left, the less likely it is to be repairable.

There are several explanations for this unwillingness to accept reality, and Figure 1.3 gives common ones.

Cause	Notes
Political	This may be internal or external, but the effect is similar, as it becomes unacceptable to admit that a disaster has occurred. In politics with a capital 'P', it is almost unheard of for a failure to be admitted – the Millennium Dome was still very much a 'white elephant' when this book was written, but few of those involved would accept this. In the UK government IT sector (home of many disasters of all sizes, but mainly huge), there is much criticism surrounding the Gateway process, which is supposed to avert disasters; much of this relates to lack of openness and political factors.
Image	The loss of face involved in admitting to the existence of the problem is too great for the responsible individuals or their managers. The negative impact on the organizations may also be unacceptable (although see also Chapter 6 on PR; it is often how the management of disaster is presented that affects the image rather than the actual disaster itself).
Ignorance	Lack of experience can lead to missing the warning signs – not questioning estimates to completion, not appreciating that time is passing but that the work is not advancing, not having a plan against which to measure progress.

Figure 1.3 Reasons for ignoring project failure

	In addition, senior management may have limited visibility of what is happening further down the management ladder and may genuinely have no idea that a project is in trouble (see Denial and Blame, below, for one explanation of why this happens).
Denial	Denial involves not being able to accept that things have got 'this bad', possibly hanging on to a false hope that things will fix themselves or that a solution will magically appear. A subset of denial is the natural tendency to understate problems when reporting to a superior, or to a client. It can be the case that something that is an unmitigated disaster at the coal face is not even an issue by the time it gets to the board of directors (until reality delivers them a surprise later on).
Blame	Refusing to accept responsibility; 'we have done nothing wrong, so if there is a disaster, then it was someone else's fault.' This is another take on denial and is one of the driving forces behind the watering-down phenomena of reporting bad news up the command chain.

Figure 1.3 Reasons for ignoring project failure (*continued*)

WHY FAILURE SHOULD NOT ALWAYS BE PUNISHED

One of the clear lessons from researching material for this book is that the 'blame culture' that is very prevalent in Western society and organizations is not conducive to a positive outcome. This is not to say that there should be no redress on organizations that are genuinely negligent, but the pendulum seems to have swung too far in the blame direction.

While it is clear that failure is not a 'good' thing, the increasing aversion to any form of risk (the other side of the blame culture's coin) must stifle innovation. There needs to be an acceptance of failure if anything new is to be tried, which by definition is not going to have a predictable outcome. Similarly, there will be no entrepreneurs if failure is too harshly punished (the current action in the UK to reduce the stigma of bankruptcy to make it more like the situation in the United States is a welcome start). In the UK, it is pleasing to note that some organizations have accepted this and are adopting a culture that is more flexible and realistic about risk, at least for research projects.

However, while there is such a focus on an insurance claim and litigation-led approach to life, it will always be difficult to provide a culture that makes it easier to recover from a project disaster. Fear of fault makes openness and flexibility and the willingness to take risk less likely. As will be seen later in this book, this is the opposite of what is required in an organization that wishes to get the best result from a project disaster.

TIME WILL TELL

It is not always the case that what seems to be a disaster now is judged to be one in the future. This is not always a comfort for those involved at the time, but is worth keeping in mind.

Example: Xerox's Alto computer

Xerox's Alto computer developed in the early 1970s included local area network technology (the term Ethernet comes from Xerox), on-screen bit-mapped editing and mouse pointing devices. This was years ahead of Microsoft and Apple. The project failed because senior management largely neglected it. However, in terms of technology it was a great success, the elements used being commonplace today. It is difficult to imagine a computing environment that is not 'WIMP'-based (windows icons, mice, and pull-down menus or pointers).

The corollary of this is that you should not be too hasty to judge success either.

Examples: The Channel Tunnel and Concorde

The Channel Tunnel is undoubtedly an engineering success, but it is unlikely to be a financial one in the near future; the level of debt involved in the construction makes the break-even horizon a little distant. Concorde is a further example where a technical success ended up as a commercial failure, though arguably because of political rather than purely commercial pressures. Sadly, she is no longer flying, though many tried to save her.

SUMMARY

In this chapter, the definition of a project and what counts as a disaster has been considered. The conclusion is less hard-edged than might be liked, but that is because it comes down to the definitions of success and failure. Kipling had words to say on the subject of success (triumph) and failure in his poem 'If'.

'If you can meet with Triumph and Disaster
And treat those two impostors just the same;'

Success and failure tend to be in the eye of the beholder (this is particularly true where there is any political judgement involved). Consequently, what is a disaster to some people at a particular point in time may not be so later with a different audience. If nothing else, this should provide a consoling straw to anyone in the middle of what appears to be a disaster.

However, this lack of a hard and fast definition misses the point: a project disaster is one that is perceived to be a disaster at the time. The people working on the project team and all those affected by it will be aware that a disaster is happening. The remainder of this book will look at causes of disasters and will examine evidence that supports the best ways of getting through them.

2

Why project disasters happen

A key factor in surviving project disasters is knowing what caused them in the first place. In this chapter, the goal is to identify the most common causes of disasters to provide the knowledge that will be needed to remedy them. Hopefully, in many cases, understanding these causes may enable them to be avoided in the first place. In an ideal world, it is always better not to have the problem in the first place.

SIX MAIN CAUSES

There are said to be only a fixed number of plots available for stories, for example 'the arrival of the stranger, the quest, the journey and so on', though there is disagreement as to exactly how many of these there are. The same is true of the causes of project disasters, though again there will be those who have slightly different views as to what these are. This doesn't actually matter too much as long as you catch everything in one category or another. The author's chosen six categories include: inadequate information, external events, unclear/wrong goals, unproven technology, inadequate resources and failures of communication and management. The last of these also includes straightforward lack of planning. The old cliché 'failing to plan is to plan to fail' is true.

Unsurprisingly, this is one of the longer chapters in the book. If the reader is to hope to survive a project disaster, it is essential to know what caused it. In addition, this chapter will offer the most entertainment for the voyeurs who have yet to find themselves in such a situation and gain amusement from the plight of others. They should remember that there are only two types of project manager: those who have been involved in a disaster, and those who will be in the future.

Key point: Reading about these causes, it will become clear that there is often interaction between these categories. This is an important point to grasp as it is unusual that there is just the one cause of a disaster; there is usually a mutually interactive chain of events. This is something that project disasters have in common with air crashes – there is seldom a single cause.

Note: See also Chapter 9 where the five Ms are discussed as potential project issues: Man (people), Machine (technology), Method (process), Material (structure), Milieu (environment).

Inadequate information

This is included as a separate entry, though in many cases it could be used to include all the other causes of failure. Take the case of unclear goals or incorrect requirements; it could be argued that these are simply examples of the project team not being in possession of sufficient accurate information to be able to deliver the desired product. However, there is a limit to what can be known, so perhaps this cause of failure is a risk inherent in any human enterprise. You can never know everything.

Example: A major civil engineering project

A major civil engineering project, costing many millions of pounds, was put together to build an underground sewer. All existing surveys were studied, and all the sources of information on the local geology were examined. Local authorities were consulted on the location of mine workings, earlier tunnels and drains and so forth. In fact, all reasonable endeavours were made to establish the validity of the route to be taken by the tunnel (and related cuttings). The project was well organized and managed by experienced civil engineers with a good track record and a sound reputation for professional competence. However, a few months after the tunnel was completed, some nearby houses had to be evacuated pending rectification of subsidence. It turned out that there was an undocumented underground stream which had become diverted by the construction work, and after a time this had undermined the houses. The only way this could have been determined was by completing the project in the first place.

External events

These include politics, natural disasters, takeover/change of ownership, company failures, international crises and so on. Sometimes, these give warning of their arrival, and sometimes they do not. By their very nature, they are outside the control of the project team and any sponsoring organization. This does not mean that there is nothing that can be done about them. The following two case studies show how an external event caused a disaster; in one case it was terminal for the project, in the other it was not.

Case study: 'Legislation'

Very early on in the author's career, he was a very junior part of a project to design a check weighing system. The purpose of this system was to help manufacturers of products such as loose-packed tea meet with proposed new legislation and to minimize the amount of 'over-pack'. The legislation was never implemented, and consequently the key driver for the demand for the project disappeared. It had been announced, timetable set, legislation drafted and briefings given to industry – but it never actually came into being (at least not in the 1980s).

Case study: Change at the top

This story is from the author's own experience when he was the manager of a project within an overall programme and was able to observe events without the full pain of being caught up in them. The programme was for outsourcing the information technology of a US financial services company. The reason for the programme was that the company had a large number of separate suppliers delivering a hodgepodge of service elements. This was perceived to be expensive both in terms of the internal effort needed to manage it and because it did not allow economies of scale to be realized. Consequently, a procurement exercise was completed to find a single supplier for the full range of services. The resulting programme to get these services in place within a six-month time frame (the transition period from contract award to start of the new service) was a significant one, but it was one that was completed. The bombshell came on the Friday before the Monday when the switch from the old suppliers to the new one was due to take place for the first (significant) phase. The client decided to cancel the entire deal on the grounds that 'the business case for the change in supply had been reviewed and was no longer considered valid'. This was quite a dramatic turn of events, and there is almost another book in how you stop a major programme at such a late stage.

There is another, more probable cause, for this disaster. The IT director who had sponsored the original decision to outsource to a single supplier left the company, and the replacement director arrived to find that the IT department was effectively being shrunk to a much smaller one. In addition, the new director had

had a very bad experience with the outsourcing supplier at a previous organization. It was this change at the top that was the real cause of the disaster, an event totally outside the control of the programme and project managers. Needless to say, the legal profession probably did better out of this than anyone else did.

Note: Regulation is an ever-increasing burden on businesses and projects. It is becoming more and more common for additional regulation to be imposed on business in the light of perceived risks. This is another consequence of litigation and the blame culture. Any project that has a direct interface to the public should keep a close watch on pending legislation/regulation.

Unclear/wrong goals and requirements

Many projects fail because they do not have sufficiently clear goals. Some fail even more spectacularly because they have the wrong goals. Having unclear goals can easily lead to problems, but to get a first-class disaster, having the wrong goals wins hands down every time. The following case study was a very high-profile project disaster in 2003.

Case study: Records system

This system had a clear overall goal: to deliver a system that could process requests for the retrieval of certain records to support job vetting (among other things) within certain time limits specified in a service level agreement (SLA). Unfortunately, owing to a poor or incomplete understanding of the nature of the requests and how they would be received, the project goals were built around the delivery of a system that would use a 'call centre' to fulfil the bulk of the requests for the retrieval of records. A primary goal was to build an efficient call centre to provide the point of contact to the clients. Sadly, this goal was the wrong one; the majority of the requests did not come in as calls that would then have been processed by the efficient call centre, but rather as paper-based forms (in the post, by fax and so forth). Although some were expected this way, and there was a process for dealing with paper-based requests, the end result was an underused call centre and an over-stressed manual processing department. The overall system was incapable of meeting the required processing volumes and turnaround times expected of it. A short-term fix was to employ large numbers of people to manually transcribe the paper-based information into the call-centre system. However, solving the real problem required significant expense and resulted in severe criticism of all concerned. Bad assumptions led to the wrong goals being set; that this was not discovered until after the service became live is possibly an even greater disaster than getting it wrong at the start.

Note: See also the chart in Chapter 3, which shows the relationship between when such a mistake is discovered and the amount of cost required to fix it.

Key point: In fact, if a project does not have measurable, well-defined goals, then it is difficult to say whether it failed or not.

False assumptions

Allied closely to the 'wrong goals' are false assumptions. In the case study above, it was assumed that most requests would come via a telephone call, and that therefore a call-centre would be the most appropriate solution. This proved to be false, and the consequences were very public indeed. However, in most projects, false assumptions give rise to delays and costs rather than outright disasters. That said, they are often found to be contributory factors; as stated earlier, disasters seldom have a single cause.

Case study: False assumptions

Although some would argue that this project was never actually a success, an example of starting afresh, at least for part of the project, was the UK's Millennium Dome. There were effectively three separate projects associated with this venture: transport, construction and contents/entertainment. The transport element was mainly associated with the extension of the Jubilee underground railway line to provide access to the Dome. This project was completed on time, though not without setbacks. The construction of the Dome also went well and was a success as far as the architectural and building aspects were concerned. However, the project that was to determine the content was fraught from the beginning, and while it eventually delivered the exhibits that were in place in time for the Millennium celebrations, the visitor numbers were not encouraging: about 350,000 in the first month, well under the estimate of about 1 million visitors a month. In February 2000, the Chief Executive and Accounting Officer left the Company, so a decision was made to employ an entertainment specialist, Pierre-Yves Gerbeau, to take charge of the project; he took over in February 2000. By this time, the original management team was largely gone, and M Gerbeau effectively started the project again. He changed the marketing strategy and approach and was able to increase the visitor numbers by 80 per cent. Sadly, this was not enough to remedy underlying financial problems, and the project had to be bailed out with additional lottery funding.

Note: At the time of writing, the Millennium Dome, unused, was costing the UK taxpayer £190,000 per month to 'mothball'; this will continue until work starts on its next evolution. It is due to become a sports arena as part of a general re-development by 2007 and would be available for the 2012 Olympic Games if London wins the right to hold them.

Requirements

Underlying problems of the right/wrong or unclear goals are the requirements the project was set up to fulfil. The driving force for defining the goals should be the requirements of the problem to be solved. Where this is not the case, it becomes a seed for disaster in all project areas.

Key point: Even when requirements are established at the time that a project is commenced, they are not necessarily true by the time the project is delivered. With requirements, it is always worth asking 'what has changed?'

Case study: Storage

This particular project disaster was a very expensive one as the cost of fixing it was £100 million plus. Special containers were to be manufactured for the storage of hazardous materials in a purpose-built facility that would include automated handling equipment. The requirements for the containers included very specific dimensions with tight tolerances to be met to ensure that the handling equipment would work correctly. The containers were correctly produced and met all tests, including size and suitability for purpose. This project was a success. By the time the containers had been produced, the facility itself had also been completed, a significant civil engineering exercise. Sadly, some internal dimensions in the facility were just a fraction too small to allow the containers to be moved around. It was a choice between replacing all the containers or rebuilding the facility – both were high-cost options. The requirements for the containers had changed by the time they were delivered.

Unproven technology

The use of unproven, or leading-edge technology (or the use of proven technology in a new field) carries with it significant risk. When doing something for the first time, or even being in the vanguard of early adopters, there are two sources of increased risk. Firstly, there are a higher than normal number of unknowns, and, secondly, there is no pool of in-depth expertise on which to draw when things go wrong.

Case study: Aviation

The de Havilland Comet 1, the world's first jet airliner, serves as a good example of where working at the leading edge of technology can lead to an unpredictable outcome. The Comet 1 first flew in 1949 and was revolutionary in terms of range and performance. It was capable of over 500 mph and could cover flights in excess of 1,500 miles. The speed was more than double that available previously, and made journeys from London to South Africa possible in less than a day. Furthermore, it operated at altitudes of up to 40,000 feet – vastly higher than contemporary propeller airliners – and was thus able to fly above the weather in uncluttered airspace, giving passengers fast and smooth journeys. In economic terms it was also attractive, as it offered almost twice as many passenger miles per pound/dollar as existing aircraft. Consequently, its impact on the airline industry in the early 1950s was marked, and orders were received for long-range, including planned transatlantic, versions. As a project, it seemed to be an unqualified success, and de Havilland was on the verge of dominating the aircraft industry.

At this point, it is important to note that the design team, led by Ronald Bishop, had ensured that all elements of the design were fully tested to the required standards, and more critically, the knowledge available at the time. One part of this testing was on the pressurized fuselage – for passengers to be able to breath comfortably at altitudes much above 8,000 feet, it is necessary to pressurize the cabin. This means that the pressure inside the aircraft is much greater than that outside. The structure needs to be able to cope with both the pressure differential and the changes in pressure as the aircraft goes from ground level to cruising height and back every flight. To this end, the Comet 1 cabin was tested to the limits of the understanding at the time, and this included pressure-testing of the cabin. In January and April of 1954, two Comet 1s suffered from what was subsequently established by investigators to be explosive decompression – the cabin failed to contain the pressure differential. Each of these aircraft had flown around 1,000 flights, much less than the 16,000 plus flights for which the design had been tested. Consequently, the Comet 1 was grounded pending further testing.

New pressure tests were carried out in a water tank (to simulate pressure changes). A feature of this was that, compared with the original pressure-chamber tests, it was possible to cycle the pressure more quickly, thus saving time. In addition, it was possible to use waterproof seals to test the cabin in combination with the wing roots (the original tests involved the cabin-pressure hull alone), making the test closer to real flight. During these tests, the cabin failed at the corner of the nearly square windows. This was the same point of failure that had been identified from studying wreckage recovered from the crashed aircraft. The failure occurred much more quickly than in the original tests and was consistent with the age of the lost aircraft. The cause of the failure was metal fatigue that made itself evident at stress points, such as the corners of the windows. The investigation had shown that establishing structural and material strengths of a design, the contemporary practice, was not a guard against metal fatigue. At the time of the Comet 1, the science of metallurgy was not sufficiently advanced to have identified metal-fatigue issues in pressurized aircraft; the project team tested the design within the understanding of the day.

Although the problems were overcome, de Havilland never recovered from the setback; despite the fact that the Comet 4 became the first jet airliner to offer a commercial service across the North Atlantic, the damage was done. Boeing now had its 707 operational, and de Havilland's lead was lost and the company never regained its market share. With the knowledge available to the project design team at the time, there was no way that this disaster could have been avoided. No project team can allow for eventualities that are not understood, and high-technology projects may fail even though everything was done that could have been done at the time. For most business-based projects, the consequences will not involve the loss of life, but it should be accepted that it is not always possible to avoid disaster. Comet derivatives are still in service with the Royal Air Force, however – a testament to the overall soundness of the concept.

Another example of unproven technology/design, and a famous one, is the RMS Titanic, built in Belfast, Northern Ireland. The watertight doors designed to protect the ship from sinking by dividing the hull into watertight compartments were not tall enough, and water was able to pass over the top of one into the next. The first time this technology was tested was in the tragic incident involving collision with an iceberg.

Note: An additional cause of failure, particularly for IT projects, is that of enthusiasm for technology outstripping the requirement and resulting in an over-ambitious design. The desire to work on a challenging and exciting technological solution can lead to the adoption of 'leading-edge' solutions that are inherently more risky than proven ones. It is often the case that a simpler, and easier, solution was available but was ignored because it was essentially dull.

Inadequate resources

Lack of resources emerged as a main or contributory cause for many of the project disasters researched for this book. Resources for projects come in three flavours: funding, people and equipment.

Funding

Underpinning any project is the money to pay for the costs that will be incurred (let alone any profit that was hoped for) in delivering it. Any project that has serious shortfalls in this area will inevitably fail – there will not be enough money to pay for the delivery resources of people and equipment. There are many possible causes for this including inaccurate estimates, changes in the project environment (again, note the interaction with external events), changes in requirements and so forth. It is often the case that the first real sign of a project disaster is a runaway in spending without a reasonable and acceptable explanation.

Sometimes, however, it may not become clear until after the project has been completed that the financial resourcing was incorrect. Take as an example a PFI (public finance initiative) project where a planned charge per transaction had been determined but then, for whatever reason, the volume of transactions expected proved to be significantly lower than that predicted. In retrospect, such a project would be seen as a disaster, but the team may well have delivered it to time and on budget.

There is also the case where the cause of the resource problem is another project that has a higher priority. Here, it may well be that one project has to fall in order for an organization to realize a higher-priority goal.

Case study: X-15 rocket plane and the Apollo Moon-landing programme

In the 1960s, President Kennedy's response to the Russian's cold war lead (real or perceived) in space technology was to state that the United States would put a man on the Moon (and bring him back) before 1970. In fact, this was accomplished in July 1969, five months before the deadline. This was a stunning achievement, but apparently it was not made without cost to other space programmes, which were either not extended or were finished early, notably the X-15 rocket plane. At the time of Kennedy's challenge, the X-15 rocket plane was already taking man to the edge of space without the use of expensive and fuel-hungry boosters such as those of the Saturn 5. It was effectively doing what Burt Rutan's SpaceShipOne had just started doing in 2004. Arguably, going to the Moon set back affordable space technology by more than 30 years, though the spin-offs and knowledge gained from this endeavour are magnificent and arguably outweigh any loss. The higher-priority project took resources from the lower-priority projects, though it is hard to describe the X-15 as anything but a success. However, it might have achieved even more if it had not been terminated when it was. Of course, it is possible to call this an example of an 'external factor' – as with all disaster-related factors, there is seldom just one cause, and there will frequently be grey areas.

Note: Related to funding in general, Nickson's *Corollary* (1998) states that 'A project sold by a professional sales team and purchased by a professional procurement team will have a combination of price, deliverables and a timetable that are impossible to achieve.' This cynical viewpoint has been borne out by reality too often to be ignored. Most commonly, it shows up in the form of an unrealistic price (and therefore project budget).

Similarly, the rule of 'two out of three'. The three components of a project are good, quick and cheap. You can only have any two of these together in the real world; getting a good, quick, cheap job is like the mythical free lunch. It doesn't happen, and any project set up on the basis of achieving something like this is well along the route to disaster.

People

People should be considered first, because personnel are more often the cause of problems than is equipment. It is not just lack of people that is the problem, however; as an expensive resource, it is unusual that there are too many people available to choose from. Having the wrong people often has a higher impact than not having the right headcount. A fully staffed project team that has people who are unsuited to working together, who have the wrong skill sets, or who require extensive training before they are productive, is a real problem.

A further issue with personnel concerns a project being allocated team members who may have the right skills but who are not dedicated to the project and have higher calls on their time. If they are regularly found to be on the critical path for the project, delays can build and build until the project fails.

Equipment

Lack of equipment can lead to major problems for a project, but it is a less common cause because equipment tends to be easier to plan for. That said, having the wrong equipment or getting it late can cause severe problems. A classic example is not having a crane available at a building site when the reinforced-concrete floor panels arrive. The consequences are that the load cannot be taken off the lorries, the workforce can make no progress, and a new delivery has to be arranged for when the crane is there. There are cases when the equipment does not work as expected, and this can be catastrophic. In general, however, equipment is not a major cause of project disasters, but it is usually symptomatic of poor management and planning.

Case study: Utilities industry

In 2003, a major European-owned utilities organization accepted a very professional bid for project management services from a reputable supplier to manage service delivery to a third party. The bid manager, a strong personality, had put forward a strong case and had demonstrated a good theoretical understanding of the project management skills needed to get the job done. However, the first project manager supplied was not a strong character, and the project was seen to be rapidly getting away from him. The supplier offered a second candidate to 'get things back on track'. Sadly, this proved harder than expected, and after less than two weeks the new manager could not be located either on-site or at the nearby hotel. It seems that, without stopping to tell anyone, this manager had abandoned ship. At this point, the utilities company demanded a better project manager to fix things, but agreed to pay extra for the right calibre of candidate. Arguably, this should have been free of additional charges, as it is clear that the staff provided did not live up to the proposal. This PM fared better and got things partially recovered before being withdrawn, presumably to meet another crisis of the supplier's organization.

A fourth PM was supplied, but (without the utilities company knowing) had been given a brief of making additional profit from the project. This resulted in some fairly heated project team meetings, where it was clear that the PM's goals were not in line with those of the overall project team. By this time, the project was in serious trouble with the client of the utilities company, who, rather than face continued losses, was forced to terminate the contract. Not counting the consequential losses to the utilities firm and time wasted by its internal staff, it also incurred severe losses from cancellation of the related contracts. The direct cause of the disaster was an inadequately qualified resource; arguably, it could be said that this was also because the utilities company failed to validate that the resource offered was up to the job to be done. The utilities company also failed to check that the communication with the supplier was fully understood and that the right specification for the project manager was being satisfied.

However, it is also somewhat unlucky to get three out of four unsuitable people for the same role.

Failures of communication and management

Failures of communication and management include misunderstandings, failure to check understanding, false assumptions, cultural mismatches, lost messages, poor planning and poor setting of objectives.

Case study: NASA Mars probe

Back in 1999, NASA was embarrassed when its *Mars Climate Orbiter* (which cost US $125 million) was lost having travelled more than 400 million miles to get there. On arrival, it flew about 60 miles closer to Mars than it should have and interacted with the atmosphere, an event it wasn't designed to cope with. This also shows the precision with which space missions have to be executed; the error amounted to less than 0.000015 per cent. The calculations for the 'burn' to get the spaceship into the correct Mars orbit were made by a team in Colorado who used imperial measures and computed the force in terms of 'pounds force'. Sadly, the team programming the computer that controlled the 'burn' used metric measurements and assumed the units were newtons. As a newton is about a quarter of a pound force, this did not produce the desired result. This error went unnoticed throughout the extensive planning, designing and testing phases of the mission – it was only in the post-mortem that it was discovered. Its effect was small, but fatal to the mission. This was both a communication error and a failure to check assumptions. Both teams were highly professional and experienced, so it shows that it is never foolish to check what might seem the most obvious points.

Note: The author is aware of one disaster where the communication error was as trivial as a lost phone call. The client had called when the project manager was out at a meeting and left a message with someone who happened to be passing through the office, and being helpful picked up the call rather than let it ring. This person took the message and wrote it down on a 'post-it' note. Unfortunately, the cleaners came round that evening and the message, which had come adrift from the phone, was put in the bin. (The organization had a clean-desk policy, and cleaners assumed that anything that looked like a scrap of paper was just that, and not significant.) The message changed a vital parameter, the total number of users, for the design, and this went un-detected for some time; the cost and time penalties to the project were considerable. It is clear that the fault lay with the client, for not checking that the message was received and recorded, but it was thought that the message had been left with a responsible person. If it is important, always check. This was in the days before e-mail was commonplace, but it is still possible for this to happen.

Estimating and planning

Estimating and planning are fundamental to any project; if there is no sensible estimate for the activities required to deliver it, then there can be no plan. Once you have estimates for the work to be done, then you need to know who, how and when. There are many different planning techniques available – GANTT charts, PERT, WBS and so forth. In essence, they identify activities (or tasks) to the level of individual responsibility and have provision for defining sequence, time frame and required resources. There is endless scope for these to go wrong, but this is generally the case because the information put into them is not correct.

The best source for examples of bad planning is any one of the television make-over and property-development programmes. Invariably, the inexperienced subject of the programme has no idea of how long things really take (or cost), is ignorant of con-straints (such as planning permission), or does not know simple sequential limitations such as getting the roof on before starting on the interior. The end result is a project that bears little resem-blance to the original plan.

Note: The trick with estimating is a simple one. The people making the estimates need to have the knowledge and experience to do so.

Setting objectives

One of the primary skills of a project manager is that of setting objectives. You cannot expect people to do a job for you unless they are clear what they are supposed to be doing; they must know what the team, and individual, objectives are. Just as many projects seem to be setting out to meet the wrong requirements; others with the right requirements are let down by poor communication of what the objectives are. There is a short acronym – SMART (simple, measurable, achievable, realistic/resource, timetable) – which allows objectives to be evaluated. 'To have your team paint the Forth Road Bridge blue by Tuesday' is simple, it is measurable (it will have turned blue), it isn't achievable using current technology, you would need immense resource not just a few workers (so it isn't realistic), and the timetable is ludicrous. This is a trivial example, but the same measurement can be applied to any team goal. Nothing demotivates people faster than being made to work hard at something that can never be completed. Objectives may be difficult and challenging, but they should be possible and clearly defined. Failure to follow such a simple rule as SMART has been a cause of project disasters.

'Group think' or 'team think'

Associated with management and leadership is 'group think'. 'Group think' or 'team think' is rather like a virus that affects apparently successful groups. It was identified in 1972 by Janis and Mann. They identified a pattern of behaviour that leads to extremely poor-quality decisions and outcomes – and eventually (although the team may not be fully aware that this is happening), the distancing of the team's thinking from the realities of their surroundings can lead to failure to meet the objectives that the team was set. The main cause of 'team think' is poor communication, both within the team and between the team and the rest of the company.

Under the following conditions, the 'team think' syndrome is likely to occur:

- where the team is very well bonded and enjoys working together;
- where the team does not get any outside criticism;
- where the team leader is particularly strong and the leadership is followed by the team;
- where the team does not make alternative plans;
- where the team does not look critically at their actions;
- where there is pressure to make fast decisions.

A horrible smugness pervades the team; any threats to the team are dismissed as not worth thinking about, silence is taken to mean consent, people actually appoint themselves as 'mind guards' and discourage any dissent or individual doubts. The pressure for the team to agree peacefully over everything is overwhelming, so much so that reality becomes uncomfortable. You can imagine what this does in the hurly burly of a project. Decisions become sloppy, risks are overlooked, the team settles comfortably into its own little world, and things begin to go wrong. A cure for 'group think' is provided in Chapter 8.

IT ISN'T ALWAYS THAT SIMPLE

It is worth making a parallel here with major accidents such as air disasters. Although in these cases the end result is clear – loss of life and a large amount of wreckage strewn all over the place – the causes are often complex and illustrate a degree of inter-dependency.

Example: Based on an actual event, the accident described in this example occurred when an aircraft, which had been chartered for the export of livestock overseas, was making a surveillance radar approach (SRA) to Runway 25 at Landaway Airport, under conditions of patchy lifting fog. The aircraft descended below the minimum descent height (MDH) for the approach procedure and collided with electricity cables and a transmission tower (pylon) which was situated on the extended centre-line of the runway, some 1.1 miles from its threshold. The collision caused major damage to the inboard high-lift devices on the left wing and the left engine, and the consequent loss of lift on the left wing, together with the thrust asymmetry, caused the aircraft to roll uncontrollably to the left. When passing through the vertical attitude, the left wingtip impacted the gable end of a house, causing major structural damage to the property. The aircraft continued rolling to an inverted attitude and hit the ground in an area of woodland close to the edge of a housing conurbation. An intense fire ensued, during which a large part of the forward fuselage aft to the wheel well, including the wing centre section and the inboard portions of the wings, were consumed. The five occupants suffered fatal multiple injuries on impact. There were no injuries to other persons.

The report identifies the following causal factors:

1. The flight crew allowed the aircraft to descend significantly below the normal approach glidepath during a surveillance radar approach to Runway 25 at Landaway Airport, under conditions of patchy lifting fog. The descent was continued below the promulgated minimum descent height without the appropriate visual reference to the approach lighting or the runway threshold.
2. The standard company operating procedure of cross-checking altimeter height indications during the approach was not observed, and the appropriate minimum descent height was not called by the non-handling pilot.
3. The performance of the flight crew was impaired by the effects of tiredness, having completed more than 10 hours of flight duty through the night during five flight sectors, which included a total of six approaches to land.

It is important to note that there is no single cause that led to this crash. If the crew had not been tired, they may well have followed standard operating procedures and checked the MDH. If the aircraft hadn't gone below the glide slope, it wouldn't have mattered that they didn't check this height.

Although there was a chain of events that led to the eventual crash, there was, in addition, a degree of interaction between the links in the chain without which disaster would have been averted. This interaction and linkage can lead to grey areas in identifying the causes of a project failure. Unclear goals can lead to incorrect resources being chosen and the wrong management approach being taken. Poor communication of what is needed by a project manager can lead to the wrong skill set being specified for team members and can lead to them being given the wrong tasks or priorities. This can then result in a need for significant changes and a timetable crisis when the consequences of this become visible. It is tempting to look at the last and largest factor as being the cause of the problem; however, this is almost always a mistake. Fixing this problem only will seldom rescue a project from disaster; another crisis will occur, probably more quickly than expected.

Key point: When looking at the root cause of a project disaster, a forensic approach is essential. There is seldom a single cause of a project disaster, but rather a chain of events that led to the visible event.

OTHER CAUSES

Although the six general categories cover most things that can cause a project to go off the rails, it is also clear that there are specific causes that rate a mention, and these are described in this section. They include: stress, legal disputes, the butterfly effect and scale.

Stress

Though usually an effect of a project disaster on a team member (or even the whole team), stress can be a causal factor. People who are genuinely suffering from stress (as opposed to just being tired or overworked in the short term) are less efficient at doing their job and can also make the rest of the team ineffective because of their behaviour.

Example: The author recently worked in the humble role of editor/document layout designer on a very large European Government proposal (the delivered bid weighed in at 250 kg – the department in question was not concerned with conservation!). The person who was immediately responsible for feeding the documents to be worked on was clearly suffering from stress (see Appendix 2). Indeed, this person did not make it to the end of the bid production process. It was very clear that the stress was making it very difficult for this person to work at anything like their normal efficiency, and the knock-on effects were considerable. Much work was repeated, and even more was unnecessary.

Legal disputes

As with divorcing couples, once legal specialists get involved in a dispute between a supplier and a client, then this can be a cause of a disaster in itself. This is not because lawyers aim to cause further damage, but because they are briefed to protect the interests of their respective clients, and this tends to become a defensive situation. In particular, serious consideration will be given to anything that might give rise to any from of damages or compensation claim. Of necessity, this leads to a significant overhead on the project; often the first step is to halt everything or insist that the legal experts give the OK for every new step, and this makes progress very difficult. In addition, once battle lines are drawn, it becomes increasingly difficult to get cooperation from either side. So, something that might have been discussed informally over a cup of coffee suddenly involves a whole raft of managers and advisers.

Note: This should not be taken to imply that project managers should not seek legal advice; in fact, a good project manager needs to have a good grasp of what the legal position is so that they understand the consequences of their actions. Take, for example, penalties for late delivery, failure to comply with health and safety regulations and so forth. However, this does not mean getting the lawyers involved on an adversarial basis until it is really necessary as a late, if not last, resort.

Butterfly effect

At this point, it is worth mentioning the 'butterfly effect' that grew out of Chaos Theory (see Bibliography for a suitable reference). In this effect, a very small event, such as overlooking a minor assumption, can lead to a major, unpredictable, effect further down the line. There is little that the project manager or team can do to stop this. The butterfly effect is a chaotic one; it happens in complex systems, where starting from the same point and doing exactly the same things will not result in the same outcome. You are more likely to be the victim of this in a very large project. It was so called because the idea was that a butterfly flapping its wings in one place could, eventually, lead to a tornado somewhere else in the atmosphere.

Scale

In addition, there are factors that apply to the scale of the projects that can make them particularly prone to disaster. This is not to say that all the other issues discussed in this chapter do not apply; they do. However, very small and very large projects have their own peculiar problems. This section looks at some of the issues that are peculiar to scale.

Small projects

On the whole, small projects are considered to be easier and less prone to disaster than are large ones. However, there is safety in numbers; if you have a project or a programme that includes hundreds, or even thousands, of staff and activities, while any one may be capable of seriously impacting the whole, there is a good chance that quite a bit can go wrong without destabilizing the entire enterprise. There is also a swings-and-roundabouts effect. Some project areas may fall behind and need additional resources, but other areas that go better than planned can balance this out. For small projects, this is not the case; almost any problem on a small project is likely to be on the critical path. At the extreme end of the spectrum is the one-person project – if they are struck down, the whole thing stops for good. In essence, with a very small project, almost everything gets to be on the 'critical path'; the impact of any failure can be more significant than in a larger endeavour.

Case study: Delivery of accounting and billing support

The following example is from early on in the author's own career. The project was to deliver accounting and billing support for a service aimed at collecting consumer gas and electricity data over telephone landlines 'off hook' (ie when not in use for telephone calls). At the time, this was new technology. The author was the part-time project manager for this work and had a small staff of one full-time and two part-time technical experts. The timetable was not aggressive, but was on the critical path for the pilot service to prove the technology and viability of the concept. The author's project was not rocket science and was seen as being low risk in terms of delivery. However, the following events occurred within the space of a few weeks. One team member's father died in Australia (the project was based in the UK), and he had to return home for several weeks. Another team member broke a leg when running for a bus and tripping – hospitalization followed. The third team member, possibly concerned at the misfortunes of his colleagues, chose to leave the company. A project team of three was reduced to zero in a matter of weeks. This was certainly a disaster as far as the project's timely progress was concerned – replacing the staff would have meant an effective project restart. Fortunately, field trials of the client's telephone-line technology had run into serious problems too, and their timetable was slipping even faster. There was time for the team to reassemble and for personnel leaving the organization to be replaced.

The key point here is that whenever you have a small project team, the uncertainties for resourcing are actually much greater than for a larger team. An analogy is with multi-engined aircraft. If you have four engines, you are four times more likely to have one fail than if you have only one engine. However, if you only have one engine, and it fails, you will not complete the journey. The saving grace is that a disaster in a small project is less likely to have significant impact on a business – there are fewer passengers onboard.

Large projects

The reader might assume from the problems of small projects that they are safer working on a large one. Sadly, this is not necessarily true. They have their own problems. The two main enemies of large projects are complexity and interdependency; indeed, surveys have shown that the larger the project, the more chance there is that it will go wrong because of this. Once a project exceeds a certain size, it can become so complex that it is not properly understood. Similarly, the levels of interdependency between project components can become so complex that understanding the knock-on effects of reasonably small problems can be limited.

Subcontractors

Large projects often involve subcontractors – third parties who are responsible for delivering a component of the overall project. They may be equipment suppliers or they may be involved with the supply of specific expertise/skilled labour. Disputes between prime contractors and subcontractors or between subcontractors can easily become the causes of project disasters.

Note: Because the plans for Terminal 5 were subject to the UK's longest ever planning inquiry (3 years and 10 months), the British Airports Authority can not afford any delays in its construction. To avoid some of the contractual problems associated with sub-contractors, the BAA has adopted a system whereby they don't subcontract risk to their suppliers for the construction of Terminal 5, the goal being to avoid disputes when something goes wrong (as, with a £1,500 million six-year project, there are likely to be a few snags). They plan to do this by having a 'let's fix the problem' approach rather than a 'my contract says X would do Y by the end of last week and they didn't' one. At the time of writing, this seems to be going well.

Plain stupidity or lack of 'common sense'

It is worth adding a small mention of being just plain stupid as a cause of project disasters. Take the following examples; all of these have happened, some many times. It is easy to laugh at them, but they keep on occurring – is your current project in this situation?

Fixed budget

The marketing department had specified a budget for developing a new product prototype (they also decided on a date, based on a planned demonstration at a trade show). The budget was woefully inadequate, and making anything that actually stood a chance of working reliably was not possible.

Fixed timetable

It was decided that a new e-mail system must be available by 4 July. This was announced by head office, and the IT department were told to make it happen. Sadly, while this was possible for the head office itself, the other offices, some of which were overseas, could simply not be reached in time.

Fixed resources

Yet again, the project under consideration was given a fixed head count (of three as it happens) and a fixed time to completion. Not only was this insufficient to do the job (it was a building project), but one of the resources did not have the relevant skills so had to learn on the job. The project overran by 100 per cent and was six months late.

Of course, there are often good reasons why organizations do stupid things; strong political and personal and competitive/commercial drivers create real pressure to deliver a project. However, when you are presented with an example of a project that is the exact equivalent of sending an airliner to a destination without any consideration of how much fuel it has on board, you sometimes wonder.

Note: Nobody asked if any of these projects were feasible (except those tasked with doing it – see also John Seddon's book *Freedom from Command and Control: A Better Way to Make the Work, Work*, which includes a cure for this sort of thing); incredible, but true.

IT PROJECTS

A chapter on why project disasters occur would not be complete without a section on information technology (IT). Troubled projects are the norm in the IT industry; partial failures are common, and disasters are too easy to find. This is particularly true in the public sector, where shifting political sands, confused messages and high levels of complexity combine to give very poor results. It is possible to find all of the causes of project failure identified in this chapter in public sector projects. It is quite believable that you could find a project here with everyone of them! Indeed, such is the level of failure in IT projects that one industry spokesperson for an organization that had a spectacular public failure shrugged it off by saying that 'every major player in the sector had an equally bad record and that they were as good as the competition.'

In part, it was IT that helped germinate the seed for this book. The author has an IT background and has seen at first hand many disasters and wondered whether this was the norm. It turned out that it is. It would have been perfectly possible to write a book purely about IT failures, though that would have been somewhat too easy a target and would not have been as much use to the reader.

In case this is seen as a qualitative assessment, the following example is summarized from a National Audit Office report. 'Fujitsu/ICL signed a £184 million contract with the government which the supplier's staff regarded as undeliverable, according to a report of the National Audit Office in January 2003 on the Libra project for magistrates courts. The project was a disaster: the main purpose of the contract was to buy a core caseworking system for magistrate's courts. A secondary purpose was to deliver office automation. In the end, the core software was not delivered but Fujitsu did supply the office automation at a cost of nearly £50 million more than the original contract price.' Furthermore, research by the Coverdale Organization found that only 16 per cent of IT projects achieved all their stated objectives. This leaves the other 84 per cent in partial or total failure. If you are not already convinced, the following quotations from RAEng/BCS report show similar findings for IT projects in the UK.

'The UK public sector alone has spent an estimated £12.4 billion on software in the last year and the overall UK spend on IT is projected to be a monumental £22.6 billion,' Basil Butler, Chairman of the working group that produced the report.

'We looked at a range of studies showing that only around 16% of IT projects can be considered truly successful.' Even conservative estimates put the cost of such failures into tens of billions of pounds across the EU. 'I wonder if the Government has assessed the risks of its latest proposal to merge the IT systems of the Inland Revenue and Customs & Excise?' asks Professor John McDermid, Professor of Software Engineering at the University of York and a member of the same working group.

So, what is special about IT; are the project managers particularly incompetent? Are the projects particularly hard? The answer seems to be that the projects are complex and the requirements are often not accurately identified at the beginning. The following quotes are taken from the author's, admittedly subjective, survey of the trade and national press relating to IT failures (note that many more examples of failures are given in the rest of this book).

Requirements that are wrong

The following quotations show that requirements are a major issue for IT projects.

'Manzur Maula, Information Director (Designate), BP, looks at the problem from an outcomes perspective. Many project managers, perhaps, are too focused on 'delivering things right' rather than 'delivering the right thing'.

Richard Mawrey QC has represented organizations in IT disputes over the past 30 years: 'Poor communication often means that IT departments and suppliers work together to develop solutions that are technically up to the job, but fail to meet the real business needs of the organization.'

Note: These quotes apply equally well to non-IT project requirements, but those quoted are from this field.

Political pressures

This is very true for government-sponsored projects – you can
have as many 'gateway' reviews as you like, but if the truth is
never accepted, then the path to failure is clear. In an interview,
John McManus, senior research fellow in the Faculty of Business
Management at Lincoln University and Professor of Management
at the US Rushmore Institute said 'IT projects are succumbing to
a form of political correctness, where no one can say bluntly that
"this won't work" for fear of upsetting the client, account manager, project manager or system architect.'

Risk management

Good risk management can make a real difference, but much of
the time it is only paid lip service to. Quoting John McManus
again, 'Most projects have a risks and issues register, but docu-
menting an issue is not the same as doing something about it.
How many risks and issues registers include factors that collect-
ively should lead to the conclusion that the project is not viable?'

Change and scope creep

Again, these are common themes; the changes requested are so
frequent and so large that the project becomes uncontrollable;
small changes in scope end up adding up to a completely different project to the one started with. This relates to the troubled UK
Child Support Agency project, for which a report stated that 'The
DWP gave EDS 2,500 requests for system changes.' It is hard to
understand how an organization could raise so many changes
and still expect the project to be delivered effectively.

Scope creep, where a (hopefully) well-defined project gets bits
added onto it in an uncontrolled manner ('Could we just add in
this?') has a similar effect. You start out with a project to design
a washing machine and then find that the specification now

requires a built-in steam iron and a tea maker (they all use hot water, don't they – it can't be that difficult?).

Legacy issues

Although not specific to IT, legacy issues, integrating with or building upon earlier technologies, can be a major problem for IT projects. In part, this is because of the potential difficulties in providing the equivalent of the existing services and the difficulties of interfacing to the existing systems. However, it also relates to potentially poor documentation of the existing systems (IT projects are notorious for skimping on the documentation when they are under pressure). This can make taking data on from the previous systems more than a little fraught. It is also easy to underestimate the level of training needed to move staff smoothly from the old to the new.

Note: Of course, poor management and planning, bad coordination of resources, and so on exist just as much, but not more, in IT as in other project industries. IT projects have more problems because they are more complex, not because they are consistently managed badly.

BEING FOREWARNED

In many cases, there are strong clues that things are going wrong. Indeed, one organization for which the author worked in the early 1980s even had a section in its project management manuals entitled 'Auguries of impending doom'. These included (with updates and borrowings from later methods):

- 'lack of understanding, or misunderstanding of objectives';
- 'staff resource plan unfulfilled';
- 'action items consistently uncompleted';
- 'client not providing information, services, etc as scheduled';

- 'changes accepted without evaluation/impact analysis';
- 'scope creep';
- 'significant packages of necessary work missing from original estimate.'

It is easy to see that these match neatly onto the causes proposed earlier; these are the symptoms that you would expect if things were going awry. For example, if a root cause was unclear goals, then you would reasonably expect that the objectives would be poorly understood. Similarly, if it was inadequate resources, then it would be unsurprising if the staff resource plan was unfulfilled. The fact that causes of project disasters have not changed with time is perhaps both disappointing and unsurprising. From time to time, these things will happen, and when not resolved, will lead to project failures or disasters.

Note: It is also worth reminding the reader that most project disasters involve more than one cause. Over time, the apparent causes may change as well. In the midst of a disaster, do not grasp at the first apparent cause and relax – there may be more.

AN ALTERNATIVE VIEW

Although the causes of disaster listed above are generally accepted as being typical for project disasters, there is an alternative view. John Seddon considers that all these causes are really symptoms of a lack of knowledge that is inevitable in a 'command and control' approach to work. His book *Freedom from Command and Control: A Better Way to Make the Work, Work* is based on a management approach developed by Taiichi Ohno, which involves looking at any organization as a system. It encourages the integration of decision making with work – those making the decisions are those with the knowledge. Decisions are not handed down a hierarchy having been made by people without the knowledge necessary to make them.

Certainly this system, or knowledge-based approach, has many merits and has developed a proven track record in a number of organizations. However, there would still be individual projects within any change programme that was brought about as a result of this approach, and the author still considers that some of these will go wrong. For example, in a radio interview, the project manager of a tunnelling company (which was making all the tunnels for the Channel Tunnel high-speed link) said that 'no matter how much you survey, how much you look at the records, you will find surprises under the ground.' You can never know everything. That said, this may well be a better approach for organizations, but it does not free them from the effects of uncontrollable external forces, and team-related problems. Having said this, it is well worth considering what Seddon said in an interview: 'Unless the top-down command-and-control-based approach to management is abandoned in favour of a systems/knowledge-based one, then there will be more and more project disasters.' It is clear that adopting such a method would significantly reduce the incidence of the wrong goals and poor communication.

Note: This systems-based approach can also be found in several of the more successful structured software-development methodologies such as Yourdan, SSADM, Jackson, Object Oriented Design and so on.

SUMMARY

There may be only a limited number of causes of disasters, but they are sufficient to generate enough problems to be going on with. If there are echoes of any of them in a project that the reader is involved with, then act now rather than later. Do not be tempted to think that the first root cause discovered is the only one; there will usually be many things wrong in a project that merits the term disaster. There is a strong analogy between an aircrash and a project disaster – it seldom has a single cause. Furthermore, it is often the case that there is interaction between the causal factors that form the chain of events that precede the disaster. It may not be possible completely to avert the impending doom, but the sooner that it is recognized and action is taken, then the better the chance of a positive outcome. Irrespective of the management philosophy or methodology that is in place, it is worth checking at least once a week to see if any bad omens are visible.

Note: For those who wish to simplify, it is arguably the case that there are only two causes of disasters: events outside the project team's control and failures of communication. This may well be true, but it isn't helpful; the specific incidents and events reported in this book should give the reader scope to be more specific in identifying causes to a level of detail that allows remedial action to be taken.

After completing this chapter, the reader may be forgiven for thinking that all projects are led by fools and knaves and that project management is a lost cause. This is by no means the case; the majority of projects at least muddle through and only a minority are real disasters. It is wrong to think the project management methodologies and disciplines are all in vain. To a large extent, it is because they are not followed or are paid lip service to that allows many of the causes identified here to occur.

Key point: Failing to learn from failure is often found as a cause of failure in its own right. This is popularly summed up in the phrase 'Those who fail to learn from history are doomed to repeat it.' Clear examples of this were the box girder bridge disasters of the 1970s; many of these had already failed in the late 1960s, but lessons were not learnt. Fortunately (in terms of loss of life), these failures tended to occur during construction, not afterwards. The most famous example of the failure of such a bridge was the Great Bridge in Melbourne, Australia, in October 1970. Earlier in 1970, a bridge of similar design had failed during construction in Wales, UK, killing four workers. Those building the Melbourne bridge ignored this failure of the Welsh bridge, with the consequence that, in October 1970, the Melbourne bridge too collapsed, killing more than 30 members of the workforce. The bridge was redesigned and was completed successfully in 1974. However, it was discovered that there were by now dozens of box girder bridges in use, and many of these needed to be strengthened.

CHECKLIST

If your project is in trouble, then start at the top of the list presented in Figure 2.1 and carry on to the end; answer every question that applies to your project. Do not be tempted to stop after answering the first question; it is probably not the only relevant one. Once this is done, then expand upon/analyse each problem item for details. If you are dealing with a disaster and don't understand the corrective action that will be required, get help from someone who does. You may not have time to learn the relevant skills yourself, but at least you now know the area of ignorance; this is step one to resolving the problem.

Cause	Yes/no
Does the project have a defined timetable, budget and set of deliverables?	
As a starting point, have the following generic causes been considered?	
– Inadequate Information?	
– External events?	
– Unclear/wrong goals?	
– Unproven technology?	
– Inadequate resources?	
– Failures of communication/management?	
In more detail, answer the following: – Would the project goals pass a SMART test (see Glossary in the Introduction and explanations elsewhere)?	
– Have they been effectively communicated?	
– Are the requirements clear?	
– Are they still valid – have they changed since they were recorded?	

Figure 2.1 Checklist: Causes of project failure

Cause	Yes/no
– Do the goals and the requirements match up?	
– Have the goals and requirements been effectively communicated? Does everyone who needs to know understand them?	
– Have all assumptions been validated and have they been challenged?	
– Have the assumptions been documented?	
– Have the consequences of key assumptions being false been assessed?	
– Is the overall scope clear and well communicated?	
– Are there signs of the scope 'creeping' without related changes to plans/resources/timetable?	
– Have any of these things changed recently?	
– Is unproven/cutting-edge technology an issue?	
– Are there enough resources (money, equipment, space, people, etc)?	
– Are they the right resources for the job?	
– Are channels of communication clear and understood?	
– Are communications working on a common basis?	
– Is there evidence of 'group think' in the team or organization?	
– Are objectives clear?	
– Is the scale of the project (too large or complex) an issue?	
– If the project is very small, does this increase dependency on individual performance unacceptably?	
– Is it an IT project? (In which case, answer all these questions again, honestly.)	
– Is the risk register and its entries realistic? (If there is not one, ask yourself why not?)	

Figure 2.1 Checklist: Causes of project failure (*continued*)

3

Learning from disasters

Although the theme of this book is that, whatever steps are taken, there will always be disasters, there is still much to be learnt from them. Learning from disasters won't stop them happening, but it will help turn the odds in your favour and will improve the chances of you surviving them. These are the reasons why this chapter has been included here. You may be lucky and never be involved with a disaster but, just as all pilots learn how to deal with engine failure even though few experience them nowadays, you are well advised to learn from those failures that have already happened. The strategies described here have all been used in the wake of a disaster by project teams, and an assessment has been made of their strengths and weaknesses. The intention is to provide the reader with the lessons that were learnt from the adoption of these strategies. Then it should be possible to review the reader's own project disaster, and its causes, before considering which of these strategies will give the best chance of a recovery. It may be necessary to adopt more than one strategy for different elements of a project.

Note: The strategies here refer solely to the project team and immediate environment. PR and HR strategies together with general and diagnostic approaches are dealt with in their own chapters.

SUMMARY OF CAUSES

As was discussed in Chapter 2, disasters have a limited number of causes; the author's view is that there are six: inadequate information, external events, unclear/wrong goals, unproven technology, inadequate resources and failures of communication and management. In addition, there is the view that the problem is more fundamental and stems from decisions being made by people without the expertise to make them; this is the 'command and control' argument put forward by John Seddon in *Freedom from Command and Control: A Better Way to Make the Work, Work*. Other causes such as stupidity, and legal action (notionally also a failure of communication or management) were also mentioned as special cases, mainly to illustrate specific points rather than as generic categories.

However, there is a significant degree of interaction between these causes, and they are often involved in a chain of events leading up to the actual project disaster. For example, not having the right goals identified for the project can lead to the wrong resources being used. This can then lead to the budget being the wrong one that was actually needed to deliver the project. Once a project has reached the disaster stage, there is seldom a single cause. On a lighter note, it is worth mentioning Nickson's *Corollary*, which states 'Any project which is sold by professional sales staff and purchased by a professional purchasing department will have a combination of specification, timetable and price which is impossible to deliver.' This gives considerable scope for multiple causes.

Note: When identifying the causes of a disaster, resist the temptation to jump on the first one found and to assume that is it. Things are seldom that simple.

STRATEGIES ADOPTED

There seem to be just three strategies available that people regularly adopt – these come down to stopping completely (abandonment), making the best of what has been done to date (salvage) and beginning all over again (start afresh). Arguably, there is a fourth strategy of just ignoring reality and pretending that nothing is wrong, but that isn't so much a strategy as self-delusion. It does happen though; indeed one cause of a disaster is ignoring the fact that things are going wrong in the first place.

Abandonment

One of the simplest strategies to adopt when a project comes to grief is just to abandon it (see Table 3.1). This may be forced upon a project team from on high. Perhaps senior management, or the project sponsor, has concluded that the situation is so out of control as to be beyond rescue or economic salvage. As a strategy, it has the merit of simplicity.

Example: Brabazon aircraft

The world is full of abandoned projects, and choosing just one has proved difficult. However, the Brabazon aircraft is a good one. In the 1940s, a British Cabinet Committee chaired by Lord Brabazon of Tara set out to determine a future course for British civil aviation. This committee came up with the requirement to build a luxurious aircraft capable of flying from London to New York and able to carry around 100 passengers, very much in the style of 'grand luxe' travel that had been the privilege of the wealthy in the pre-WW II days of the great flying boats. The intention was to build upon the proven expertise of aircraft designers who had been producing fighter-bombers, and this was particularly true for the Bristol Aircraft Company. The result was a project at Bristol, led by Leslie George FRISE BSc, FRAeS, which started in the mid-1940s. Powered by the successful 18-cylinder Bristol Cen-

Table 3.1 Abandonment of projects

Benefits	Disadvantages
A simple clean break draws a line under the proceedings and allows everyone to get on with their lives. The new project is not burdened with the baggage of the failed one.	Those involved may well consider that they have failed or that they have become associated with failure. At the very least, they will have nothing to show for their efforts.
Stops the throwing of good money after bad. No further resources are wasted, and they can be re-deployed where they can do something useful.	Everything done to date is wasted; this applies to resources, both time and money.
Analysis of why the project had to be abandoned can provide useful lessons for the future. It may be possible to re-use some elements of completed project work elsewhere, though this is not often the case.	Nothing is delivered to the organization; there are no benefits that will be realized. This assumes there was a good reason for the project in the first place (a possible cause of disaster is that there is sometimes an absence of goals to meet).
A fresh look can be taken at what is actually needed; any follow-on project can be given goals that pass the SMART test and deliver what the organization needs.	Where the requirements were real, then a new project will be needed to deliver them. More time will be wasted whilst any new projects/ teams are set up.

taurus, the aircraft was to have a 177 ft fuselage with a 230 ft wingspan. With eight engines, four pairs built into the wings and driving eight paired contra-rotating propellers, this was to be a massive aircraft that would be pressurized and carry relatively few passengers in total comfort. With space for lounges and bars in addition to spacious seating, by the standards of the day the aircraft was to be huge; its appearance was much more of a shock than the later Jumbo was – there was simply nothing that big around (except possibly Howard Hughes' seaplane, the Spruce Goose, and that never really flew properly). It is worth noting that the wingspan is still wider than that of most modern airliners.

Intended to fly in 1947, the first actual flight was in 1949; by the time the Brabazon was ready for service, it was realized that the marketing was all wrong. The need was for cheap, fast travel by jet. The de Havilland Comet started delivering this in the early 1950s, and Boeing's 707 and 747, and then the Airbus A 380, have developed the concept further since then. The Bristol Brabazon Type 167 was abandoned in the mid-1950s before a Mark II version could be produced; it never entered service.

Key point: All project goals should be able to pass the SMART test (simple, measurable, achievable, resource, timetable [see Appendix 1 Teams]). Admittedly, if this had been the case with the Bristol Brabazon, it is less likely that the project would have become a disaster in the first place.

Salvage

Here the approach taken is to save any parts of the project that have worked out reasonably well (see Table 3.2). Perhaps this is analogous to not 'throwing the baby out with the bath water' when the original project is wound down. It can also be likened to 'picking over the bones' – a less attractive image but one that may convey how those involved feel about things.

Example: Beagle 2 Evolution

What promises to be an excellent example of salvage is *Beagle 2 Evolution*. *Beagle 2* was a high-profile project to place *Beagle 2*, a robotic laboratory designed to look for life, on Mars. The £45 million lander was scheduled to put down in a near-equatorial region of the planet known as *Isidis Planitia* on 25 December 2003. Sadly, despite many attempts to locate the probe, no sign of it has been found, no signal has been heard, and neither has any wreckage been observed. The reasons why this project failed were the subject of a House of Commons science and technology select committee report which said that a failure by the UK government to commit funds early enough had undermined the project's

Table 3.2 The salvage approach

Benefits	Disadvantages
Waste of money/equipment/human resources can be reduced.	There can be a considerable overhead in sorting through the remnants of the project in order to determine what might be salvaged.
It may be possible to deliver a subset of the project within the original timetable. This can have significant benefit to the morale of those involved and builds the organization's confidence in the team's ability to deliver.	Any change in delivery scope can leave the organization without critical elements from the project that may still be required. The team can still be perceived as having failed to deliver those items.
Experience gained by team members can be capitalized on; they should be in a position to prevent the same mistakes being made again.	Team members from the original project may be part of the problem and they may also become understandably defensive. It can be difficult to mix people from the original and the new project team.
The investment in establishing the reasons for the project is saved. However, these reasons should be revalidated. Keep in mind that a common cause of failure is having the wrong project goals.	The fact that time has passed can mean that the original project goals, even if they were valid at the time of commencing the project, may no longer be the right ones for the organization.

credibility. Dr Ian Gibson MP, chairman of the select committee of MPs that produced the report, said: 'The European Space Agency and the UK wanted a Mars lander on the cheap. The Department of Trade and Industry should have been on the pitch getting involved, rather than cheering from the touchline and coming on as a second-half substitute when things went wrong.' The report went on to say that the £25 million of taxpayers' money that science minister Lord Sainsbury put towards bailing out the lander was money well spent.

However, the report emphasized that the necessary funding was not there at the beginning, when it was most needed. Consequently, to quote Professor Pillinger 'The scientists had to go chasing celebrities for sponsorship when they might have been testing rockets.' Professor David Southwood, the European Space Agency Director of Science at the time, was quoted by the BBC as saying 'The view that things ought to be done differently in future comes across very clearly and that it should be done in a more integrated manner under ESA leadership. That is something I wholeheartedly subscribe to.' It had been identified what had been done wrong, and established that much had been done right. This was particularly true in terms of giving a good PR image to British space science.

So it was no great surprise when, in November 2004, the first announcements were made of a follow-up project aimed at building upon the lessons learnt, or 'salvaged', from the original project. The team has approached NASA with a view to hitching a ride on its Mars Science Laboratory, due to reach Mars in 2009.

It is an interesting PR point to note that, at the time of writing, the new project was not being called *Beagle 3*, but *Beagle 2 Evolution*, underlining the fact that it is a continuation of the original project; it builds upon the good work that was done in the 'failed' *Beagle 2*.

Start afresh

There is a traditional Irish saying that refers to asking the way to some place, with the reply 'If I were you Sir, I wouldn't be starting from here.' If the reader is currently in the middle of a project disaster, then this could well sum up the current situation. Starting again from scratch can get the project going from the right place (see Table 3.3).

Example: The new Wembley football stadium

The new Wembley football stadium is under construction as this book is being written and promises to be an impressive venue.

Table 3.3 Starting afresh

Benefits	Disadvantages
Starting from scratch provides the opportunity to redefine the project and make a better-informed second attempt.	Much of the work done to date may be lost, though it is a good idea to save anything completed or part completed for the time being in case it is useful for the 'new' project. This will be a judgement call for the project team.
A more realistic timetable can be set, possibly benefiting from lessons learnt from the project disaster (it may well be that an unrealistic timetable was a contributory cause).	Time is required to stop a project and to restart a new one. If completion by a fixed date was critical, for example time to market, then this option will probably deliver too late.
A more realistic project budget and goals can be set; the SMART test can be applied.	To stand a reasonable chance of identifying the right goals, resources and timetable effort need to be invested first. This furthers delays the achievement of the goals and, of course, costs money.
Where a contributory cause was either the wrong, too little or too much resource, then this is an opportunity to get it right this time.	New project resources will need to be identified and acquired, probably from scratch.

However, there were several false starts before this project finally got going in its current form. Plans for the new national stadium were beset with delays, management problems and spiralling costs since it was decided to redevelop the old Wembley site in December 1996. The first designs were unveiled in 1999; however, there was a major argument about whether the complex should include a running track for athletics events. At this stage, it became necessary to 'start afresh' with a new design that met the requirements of the many interested parties. This was not completed and agreed on until 2002, when the project finally got underway. The stadium is scheduled to open in 2006.

Example: The Channel Tunnel

Perhaps the longest-running example of using the start-afresh approach was the Channel Tunnel (also known by the operator's name, Eurotunnel). This is interesting because the reasons for failure were different each time. The first suggestions for a tunnel were in the early 1800s, when it was suggested to Napoleon as a mechanism for invading England. Sadly, war put paid to this idea. In fact, the necessary technology did not exist, and it would not have been possible to turn the concept into reality. By the 1880s, things had moved on. People such as Brunel had developed tunnelling technology, and the geology under the Channel was better understood. What is more, England and France were not actually at war. In 1881, the French and the English started digging (using tunnelling machines that would still be recognisable as such today) towards each other. All went well for a couple of years, then politics took a hand; the British did not trust the French not to invade, so the work ceased. During the First World War, the military expressed some regret at the lack of a supply line to the trenches directly from England. However, the powers that be still didn't trust their Continental friends, so it was not until the 1970s that it was tried again. This went well, but the 'pound in your pocket' and other economic crises stopped work again. The latest, and technically successful, attempt was made in 1987 and resulted in the present rail tunnels. Time will tell whether this will become a financial success as well as a technical one.

COST OF CHANGE

Although generally well known, the fact that uncontrolled change has been seen as both a signpost to disaster and a symptom of failing projects suggests that the increasing cost of implementing a change later rather than sooner in the project lifetime is a concept worth discussing. It is clear that this is something that must be learnt, if it is not already known. Figure 3.1 shows the cost of making a change against the lifetime of the project.

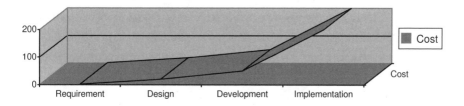

Figure 3.1 Cost of change vs project timetable

This graph serves both for changes and for fixing faults. It costs many times more to make a change once the project is nearly completed than it does at the beginning. At the requirements stage, the cost of making a change is relatively low as it is largely a paper exercise. During the design phase, the costs increase, but relatively slowly, mainly because a change in one item will require the re-working of other parts of the design, not just those directly relating to the changed requirement. Once the project gets to the development and implementation stage, however, costs ramp up dramatically. Imagine the costs of making a change to 500 point of sale terminals once they have been installed in shops across the country versus the cost of changing the (for the sake of argument) keypad layout before any units have been manufactured.

Example: European building project for a house overlooking the Mediterranean

The problem here is choosing an example, as there are so many from which to choose. This one is taken from a European building project for a rather splendid house overlooking the Mediterranean. It was discovered that although the design was exactly what the client required, it had been built exactly 90 degrees anti-clockwise to the plan. Consequently, instead of the front of the house being south facing, it was actually east facing. This was not discovered until after the foundations had been 'set in cement' and some of the walls built to the first-floor level. The cost of rectifying this was so great that there was considerable debate about what to do, and who was going to pay for it.

Related to this is the potential effect of change upon reliability. The later a change is left, the more likely it is to cause reliability problems, at least for the time it takes to settle down again. This can be seen in upgrade projects; a Government department lost access to 80 per cent of its IT systems for more than 24 hours after an upgrade went wrong. Another Government IT system, which had been the subject of more than 2,500 change requests after the initial specification was defined, unsurprisingly suffered cost overruns and did not deliver what was needed to do the job in hand.

The lesson to be learned from such disaster stories is that change needs to be kept under control. However, that does not mean having a change-control process but rather getting a grip on what is needed in the first place and getting the changes in as early as possible. Any temptation to rush the requirements and design stages in any project must be strongly resisted.

Key point: If a fault is fixed early, it will be cheaper than doing it later – for example it costs far more to recall a million cars after they have been sold than to fix the problem before the production run has started.

FALSE ALARMS

Another lesson worth learning before it happens to your project is that of false alarms. Most projects have a start date and a completion date that are well defined. There may also be payment-triggering stages where specific deliverables, for example a detailed specification or delivery of equipment, must be completed. These will often be included in the contract for the project and have a legal status. Penalties may be made for late delivery against these scheduled deliverables. These can be said to be real deadlines, though in many cases there will be scope for negotiation around these dates and their components. In addition to these, most non-trivial projects will be made up of a hierarchy of sub-projects, work packages and activities. How these are organized and planned for is a topic for project management books, some of which are listed in the Bibliography. There are many methodologies and disciplines that can be followed, but they all involve some form of breakdown of the project into simpler, understandable tasks. Along the way, critical points, sometimes known as milestones, will be identified against which the progress of the project can be measured. It is these, internal, milestones that can lead to a project being seen as a disaster when it is simply having problems. Indeed, a project team, or management, can get so focused on these milestones that they lose sight of what they are really for and the fact that they may just be telling you to review and replan. Don't let false alarms create a disaster where none exists; it can be a self-fulfilling prophecy.

Example: a Government-funded project

The author was a project manager on a Government-funded project. The project had significant customer deadlines, mainly linked to demonstrations of the system as it developed that included training sessions. It also had critical internal deadlines that needed to be met so that the client deadlines could be prepared for. Because the project had a high profile within the organization, and because there had been problems with the technical team, there was a tendency for panic to set in if any of the internal deadlines looked to be at risk. In reality, as long as the system demonstrated the correct functions so that the training and demonstration staff could prepare their work, minor, or even major, bugs in the implementation were not totally critical. The project suffered some major interference from senior management who had been alerted to the technical problems, but these would never actually have caused a project disaster. However, because senior management interfered, they nearly caused a disaster. The individual in the team who involved senior management did not appreciate the difference between an internal, manageable deadline, and a client one. The project was successful, but was, at one point, seen as being a potential disaster for no good reason. It can be argued that this was just a communication problem, but the core problem was lack of appreciation of the difference between a real and a progress-monitoring deadline.

Key point: Is your deadline a real, client-driven or immovable one, or is it a false deadline which is just a progress measure and moveable?

SUMMARY

From learning from the different techniques that have been tried when a project disaster has occurred, it becomes easier to make an informed choice about your own project disaster. Of the strategies discussed, most people interviewed seemed to feel that some form of salvage was the better option. Whether this is because it is a better strategy is hard to say. It may be the case that abandonment and starting again are often politically very unsatisfactory options – even if they might prove to be the better ones in reality. It would take a very openly cultured organization to take either of these courses of action. Consequently, it may be the case that many projects are salvaged when a better option would have been to put them out of their misery. It is also clear that keeping a lid on change once the requirements and design stages are completed is a sound plan, so do not allow these stages to be rushed. Related to this are the problems associated with false deadlines; internal organizational needs must not be allowed to cause a project to be rushed – the only real deadlines are those of the client.

CHECKLIST

Answer the questions listed in Figure 3.2 for your project and take corrective action as needed. If you are dealing with a disaster and don't understand the corrective action that will be required, get help from someone who does. You may not have time to learn the relevant skills yourself, but at least you now know the area of ignorance; this is step one to resolving the problem.

Question/comment	Yes/no?
Have <u>all</u> the causes of the project disaster been identified? - inaccurate information? - external events? - unclear goals and/or requirements? - unproven technology? - inadequate resources? - failures of communication and management?	
Are you guilty of doing nothing and hoping for the best?	
Have the following strategies been considered? - abandonment, where the goal is to avoid sending good money after bad? - salvage of specific/useful elements, either within this project or for use in another? - starting afresh rom a better position, with more reasonable/better understood goals?	
Has the increasing cost of change with time been taken into account when completing the specification and design stages?	
Is the concept accepted or understood that an early change is less expensive to make than a late one when developing a project?	
So, has the requirements/design stage been rushed?	
Do the requirements pass the SMART test?	
Is change under control?	
Are you sure that your alarms are real ones? Is a deadline a real or an artificial one?	

Figure 3.2 Checklist: Corrective action

4

Risk and reality

Risk management is one of the main techniques deployed to try and reduce the chances of a project disaster. What is more, when used effectively, risk management can significantly reduce the chances of disaster and can be used to identify, in advance, what to do when a disaster does occur. As such, no apology is made for providing an overview of risk-management practice even though many readers will be familiar with it. For those not familiar with risk-management practice, it is hoped that this chapter will act as a very basic introduction that gets them started in the right direction. There are many books, methods and courses available on the subject, but in line with the philosophy of this book, the reader will not have time to take a course in the midst of a disaster. Risk management really does help, and because of the way it is commonly applied, there will be those who miss the elements that can be useful in helping to get through a disaster.

OVERVIEW

Risk management typically follows four stages in an iterative process. These are identification, assessment, planning and monitoring. They should be followed at project start-up and then monitored in response to change, completion of project stages, and so forth. It is worth noting that one of the main reasons why risk-management activities fail to deliver as well as they should is because they get treated as a one-off exercise. Once the full heat of the project battle is underway, the risk register, plans and contingencies get left to gather dust on the shelf. This is a sad waste; the initial assessment will have helped identify where the project is most at risk and will have helped focus attention on how to mitigate these risks (or accept them). However, the lack of monitoring allows new risks to emerge, or old ones to grow more serious, without anyone actually noticing. It then comes as a surprise that the roof has fallen in on the project. Figure 4.1 shows areas where risks fit in a typical project environment.

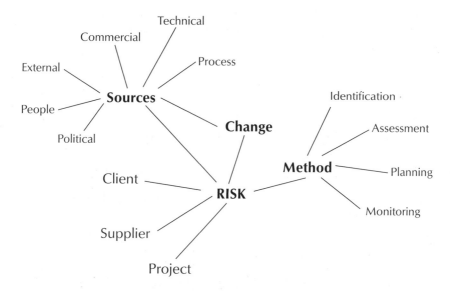

Figure 4.1 Areas where risks fit in a typical project environment (Mind Map® is a Registered Trade Mark of the Buzan Organization Ltd)

Note: There are a number of formal risk methodologies in existence; the simple overview offered here serves to show what is typically needed, but is not intended as a methodology itself. The Bibliography lists a number of books on the subject for future reading or research. Organizations such as the PMI, APM and so forth have different naming conventions and methods for dealing with risk – readers are encouraged to research the ones in use in their own organization, or indeed others, for comparison.

Identification

Identification is the first step. Ideally, it involves asking anyone and everyone (within reason) to identify any risks they consider might apply to the project, and rating them according to severity and probability. Normally, this is done on the basis of low, medium or high for both categories. These are then usually compiled into a risk register. A typical example is shown in Table 4.1.

Table 4.1 Identifying and ranking risks (L=low; M=medium; H=high)

Risk ID#	Impact (L/M/H)	Probability (L/M/H)	Description
TAX1	Low	High	Changes to tax rates during project
TAX2	High	Low	Cancellation due to change in laws relating to tax
TAX3	Medium	Medium	Late delivery of new computers

The allocation of probability and impact at this stage is usually subjective, though guidance will be given as regards impact. For example, 'low' may be described as having less than 3 per cent impact on budget or timescale for the overall project. 'High' might be defined as having greater than 30 per cent impact and so forth. Of course, it is acceptable to have more levels, but three keeps it simple for our purposes.

Note: the existence of such a risk document and the requirement for the collation/maintenance of the information to go into it implies that someone needs to 'own' it and that there is a project overhead associated with it. Many projects start out well, but then abandon proper risk management 'because there isn't time'. They often do this with documentation too – these projects are more likely to fail.

Assessment (analysis)

Methods vary as to what happens next, but in general the following is typical; it is based on ranking the risks according to combined impact and probability. The first filter employed is usually to eliminate all the 'low-low' risks. These need only be considered if their ranking changes in the future (it is not safe to simply 'file and forget' risks). The ranking process can then be applied to give increasingly higher profiles to high-impact/probability risks.

During this assessment process, it is usual to associate/review ranking numbers with the impact on budget and time. This can then be used to keep a track of how risks evolve with time as a result of project progress, risk reduction and contingency plans, plus events in the outside world.

Key point: There is often a grey area in respect of risks that have a very high impact, but a low probability. Their impact may be catastrophic, but it becomes debatable as to what extent they should be planned for if the probability is very low. Do you allow for nuclear war? Usually not, so this is an easy one – particularly as the team is unlikely to have the project's welfare as its highest priority in such an event! However, this identifies the real problem for risk in terms of preventing disasters – it is a judgement call, not a science.

Note: There are many more complex and comprehensive ways of assessing risks; some even involve statistical methods.

However, further investigation into these is left as a research opportunity for the reader.

Planning

Following on logically, once the nature of the risk has been fully assessed, the next step is to develop a plan for dealing with each risk. These typically include: ignore it, take mitigating action to reduce the chance of it happening or minimize the impact, and have a contingency plan in case it actually comes to pass.

At this stage, an entry in the risk register might look something like Table 4.2.

Table 4.2 Risk register (L=low; M=medium; H=high)

Risk ID#	Impact (L/M/H)	Probability (L/M/H)	Description	Mitigation/plan
TAX11	Medium	Medium	Changes to tax rates during project	Lobby Minister for no change via steering group; develop fall-back plan for implementing new rates.

Note: An alternative approach involves having a risk plan for every component of the project plan. Rather than using the classical risk-gathering, assessment and planning approach on a project/client-wide basis running in parallel with the project, this approach takes every element and looks at the risks that might adversely affect their completion.

Monitoring

As mentioned in the overview, monitoring is the part of the process that most often gets left out, together with failing to implement identified mitigating actions. The risk identification, assessment and planning stages need to be re-evaluated when things change. This can either be done by having regularly timed reviews (with the overhead that you might have reviews when you don't need them). Alternatively, risk reviews can be implemented whenever there is a request for a change, however trivial, or by setting criteria that determine the extent of the reviews according to the extent of the change.

The perils of missing out on this element are that new risks and the changing impact/probability of identified risks get missed. It is of little compensation to dust off the risk register after the event and say that 'we considered it, but it was a low probability at the time.'

Summary of four stages of risk management

In many organizations and methodologies, this process will have varying degrees of formality and management associated with it. There are some companies where risk management is seen as the principal tool of project management. The important thing is that risk management can help identify potential causes of project disasters, and as such is worth doing, not just at the start of the project, but through until the end. However, in terms of disaster prevention and control, the weakness is that the assessment of risks comes down to subjective evaluation. Risk management only works if it applied honestly and regularly updated – paying lip service just does not work.

Key point: The first risk that should be addressed is 'What is the impact of the project having the wrong goals?'

SOURCES OF RISK

When reviewing the causes of project disasters, the point was made that there are a number of ways you can cut the cake and an arbitrary, though generally accepted, set of causes were identi-fied. This is much the same for sources of risk. The primary sources chosen here are: commercial, technical, people, political, process and change. Table 4.3 shows how these might be related to the causes of disasters identified in Chapter 2.

Table 4.3 Relationship between sources of risk and causes of disasters

Causes of disaster	Sources of risk
Inadequate information	People, process, change
External events	Political, change
Unclear/wrong goals	People, process, change
Unproven technology	Technical, change
Inadequate resources	People, commercial, technical, change
Failures of communication and management	People, process, political, change

It is interesting to note that people come up in four out of the six categories, but change affects all of them. It is worth keeping in mind that one of the people consulted during the research for this book recommended asking 'what has changed?' at the beginning of every day (and after every meeting and so on). Table 4.3 supports the value of that advice.

Short descriptions for each of these sources of risk are given here to illustrate them more clearly.

Commercial

As with most things in the contemporary world, money matters, and financial problems can be the root cause of serious issues for a project. Financial stability of suppliers and customers is always an issue. Take as an example the situation where a supplier goes bankrupt. By the way, this may be because one of their customers has unexpectedly been unable to pay them, so it may not be easy to spot. At best, the goods/services that are needed will be delayed whilst another supplier is located; this alone can be a major headache. More likely, some money will already have been paid to the supplier, and this will be lost to the project/organization until after any liquidation process has been completed. This can take years, so may be effectively lost for the project's lifetime (and probably only a percentage will be recovered).

Other commercial risks include currency and commodity price fluctuations. These can have a significant impact on the project's financial case and are outside the direct control of the project team.

Technical

The risks associated with technology are most often those associated with it not working as advertised or not being available on time. Sometimes, the individual components work just fine, but won't work together. The end result is the same – the project is delayed, under-delivers or fails altogether. The technical knowledge needed can be affected as a consequence – the original technical team may well find that new skills are required as a result of unforeseen technical issues. Unproven technology should be treated with caution; it is one of the major causes of project failure. When looking at technology, consider not just the equipment and tools but also the maturity of the knowledge within the organization that is available to support the project team.

People

Without wishing to give support for anyone promoting a blame culture, it is a sad fact that the people who work on a project, or are 'stakeholders' for it, are among the biggest sources of risk. They can leave, they can get sick, they can go on strike, they may not have the skills or experience needed to do the job, there may not be enough of them, the team may not work effectively, they can make mistakes and so forth. Again, consider the small project example given in Chapter 2. The team was very small and, with the exception of the part-time project manager, all the key staff became unavailable for extended periods of time due to injury, bereavement and leaving the organization (possibly to avoid the run of bad luck). It should be noted that such risks are easy to identify, but are much harder to plan/mitigate against. This project was unreasonably unlucky. As the organization was large, it was reasonable to accept this risk as it seemed logical to assume that the organization could either afford temporary resources or could provide resources from elsewhere – though that of course does not solve continuity issues or team-building considerations (see also Appendix 1).

Political

This comes in two flavours. Politics with a capital 'P', ie national or local Government, can have a huge impact, but is not very likely to be influenced, let alone controllable, by the project team. The classic example of this is where Governments pass legislation that vitally affects the viability or direction of a project. International politics can play a part here too. For example, an international trade embargo can destroy the financial case for a project overnight. Fortunately, most changes driven by Politics with a capital 'P' take some time to come to fruition, so the observant have little excuse for being completely surprised by them. Politics with a small 'p', ie corporate and office politics, are more likely to crop up as surprises as they are often harder to detect and plan for. For example, one project with a multi-million pound price-tag was doomed after the finance director who had sponsored it left the organization and was replaced with a new director who was antagonistic to the supplier's organization. The project was cancelled at the last minute, after contracts were signed but just before delivery. Awareness of the problem grew towards the end as those directly involved found minor snags being built up into major issues by those higher up the organization. The end result was, of course, profitable for the legal profession but detrimental to both the supplier and the client. Politics also spills over into the project world where project team members are drawn from competing parts of the same organization.

Note: A company takeover will invariably have political implications for any projects that are in progress, usually negative. A takeover will often affect commercial risk too. Again, note the interactivity and overlap between categories.

Process

This comes down to the smooth operation of the organization's bureaucracy, or lack of it. Projects can suffer from the inability to get decisions made and documented, the time taken to get a purchase approved, even the time needed to get a PC hooked up to the e-mail system. Some processes can make it difficult to operate the financial requirements of the project where one part of the organization requires different accounting practices to another. Where a project interacts with an organization's day-to-day operations, there can be a significant overhead in procedural maintenance. For example, an organization that has a quality-system approval, perhaps along the lines of ISO 9001, may well find that keeping the approval valid costs more than the actual project. Of course, this does not mean that the quality process needs to be abandoned, but it does mean that its costs need to be included in the assessment of the project's overall worth.

Change

Finally, a common source of risk for every project or programme is change. There is a military saying that 'no plan survives contact with the enemy.' This is also true in the civilian arena: 'no plan survives contact with the real world.' Consequently, change is inevitable in all but the smallest of projects. In fact, it is fair to say that the only reason any of the sources of risk described above become real is when they change. The risk of a supplier becoming insolvent is only an issue when it happens; this may be a self-evident truth, but it should not be forgotten. So, it is reasonable to say that change is itself a source of risk. This is why project management methodologies include risk assessment as part of their change-control mechanism. At a more subtle level, time passing also implies change. One of the sources of project disasters identified in Chapter 2 was that 'requirements that are established when a project is begun are not necessarily still true by the time the project is delivered.' It is all too easy for a project team to beaver away for months only to find that what they have produced is no longer what the client requires. This usually results in contractual arguments, but the real problem was the failure to monitor change. When considering change, it is important to note that as a project continues, the risks associated with change increase disproportionally. A change during the requirements stage of a project may have cost and risk implications for the future, but will have relatively little impact in the short term. A similar change request made once the project is nearing completion has the potential for high levels of both risk and cost.

Internal/external

It can also be helpful to identify risks according to whether they are internal or external. External risks are less likely to be within the control of the project team. This split has already been identified for political risk factors in the previous section.

However, there are some factors that can only be considered as external risks. These include acts of terrorism and natural disasters, all the way through to power cuts and traffic jams. Don't underestimate the effect of the seemingly trivial. The author knows of a bid in the 1970s for a major Government project that was rejected (it was a large infrastructural project) because the proposal did not get delivered on time owing to the taxi it was in getting stuck in traffic and arriving too late. In the end, this disaster was averted on appeal, partly because the Government department concerned needed enough bids to choose from! However, it is a safe bet that research by the reader would be able to come up with an equally trivial cause of a project disaster.

Note: All these different sources of risk can overlap; for example, a political issue may result in the deliberate blocking of a decision by manipulation of 'process'. The time taken to get an approval process completed for, say, a new technician for the project team can mean that the requirements have changed, and so on.

WHERE IT CAN FALL DOWN

In disasters, what often happens is that the low-risk, high-impact items get left out on the grounds of pragmatism or available cost, and those items that were missed altogether, turn round and bite the project team. Not being realistic about risks and failing to monitor them are also common causes of problems later on. In addition, you cannot know everything; however well the risk method is followed, there is still some scope for chaos, and all you can do is minimize this.

What you do know, but ignore

The second area where risk management falls down on a regular basis comes from a natural desire to water-down bad news. The following example gives an idea of what is meant here.

Example: The engineer told the team leader that her activity (on the project's critical path) would be at least three months late because a supplier had delivered the wrong equipment, and that was the lead time for making the new parts. The team leader told the project manager that 'it looked like there would be a few weeks delay, but we're doing all we can to pull it back.' The project manager told the departmental head that 'there might be a short delay, but we can probably work round it.' The departmental head had lunch with the Chief Executive and said 'Things are just fine.' (*Note*: See also 'Giving bad news' in Chapter 9).

This also happens with risk; things get watered down – an unreasonable timetable may well end up as having an entry in the risk register something like Table 4.4.

Table 4.4 Example of an unacceptable risk-mitigation entry (L=low; M=medium; H=high)

Risk ID#	Impact (L/M/H)	Probability (L/M/H)	Description	Mitigation/plan
TIME1	High	Medium	Timetable for activity too short	Monitor the situation

In Table 4.4, what is really very serious for the project has a minimal description and a very unsatisfactory mitigation/plan associated with it. What does 'monitor the situation' do to help reduce the risk, or mitigate its impact? Have a look at a few risk registers and see how many cases are like this. If a project is in trouble and the risk register is full of such entries, don't be too surprised, and try and do something about it; it may not be too late.

What you don't monitor

Even in organizations that have a first-rate methodology for risk management, there can still be a tendency to treat it as a one-off exercise, or to discard risks too early and fail to reconsider them as time passes. Both these failings can lead to bad news later on. Few people, if any, set out to do either of these things on purpose; most methodologies and training courses go out of their way to prevent this. However, once a project is underway, and particularly if it is under pressure, monitoring risks, like documentation, is one of the easiest things to consider you can do without. This is invariably a mistake; there are examples of very public failures where the subsequent enquiry has shown that the cause (or causes) of the catastrophe were identified in the early risk-identification stages, but that once things got underway they were conveniently forgotten. The same applies to monitoring the risks; in an earlier chapter, the benefits of asking the question 'what has changed' at the start of every day and at every meeting were extolled. This should be the motto of the person responsible for risk management in a project. Low-probability, high-impact risks have a nasty habit of coming back later on with a higher probability of risk than is comfortable for the safe delivery of the project goals.

Key point: Risk management will only work if it is done properly and not merely paid lip service to.

Example: The author worked as a project manger at an organization that was keen to sell its services to its client beyond the feasibility stage. Any risks that were identified that senior management thought might prejudice this were ruthlessly suppressed in the delivered risk plan. To all intents and purposes, the risk plan that was documented was simply an exercise to produce a deliverable, not to reflect the real situation. There are some who consider this a reasonable tactic, provided that the organization keeps a realistic assessment for its own use, particularly when costing. It is the author's view that this deception can come back and bite the supplier in the leg later on if it is discovered by the client, possibly due to a high-risk element coming to pass.

Note: Related to this is the sales technique whereby risks that impact a competitor organization's bid more than your own are highlighted to bring them to the attention of the client. This is less risky than the earlier example as it does not mean leaving things out.

What you don't know

There is a popular analogy used in 'pop' psychology called the Johari Window based on a concept by Joseph Luft and Harry

Ingham (see also its mention in Chapter 2 on causes of disasters). This was originally used to analyse personal communication. However, when restated in general terms, it offers the truism that there is always something you don't know about that can come and bite you in the leg.

Know you know	Don't know you know
Know you don't know	Don't know you don't know

Figure 4.2 What you don't know

Figure 4.2 shows the four areas of knowledge and ignorance and relates them to the individual's (or the project team's as a whole) awareness of their knowledge. Of course, it is interesting to consider all the things we 'don't know we know', such as instinctive understanding of body language, without ever having been taught it. However, it should never be forgotten that there are always things that we don't even know we don't know too, and these can never be eliminated as a potential cause of a project failure.

For example, the author heard a programme on BBC Radio 4 that included an interview with the man responsible for all the tunnelling work involved in building the high-speed rail link between the Channel Tunnel and London. In this interview, it was explained that everything was surveyed very carefully and that all existing maps, details of mining activity and so forth were taken into account before any digging was done. He made it very clear that despite this, you just couldn't know everything; the work went off well, except for a number of back gardens being damaged as a result of unrecorded weaknesses in the ground. You cannot know everything!

Case study: High-speed Channel Tunnel–London rail link

A UK-wide roll-out had been planned well in advance in order to ensure that all the logistics, including equipment, spares, transport and so forth needed to support the installation team would be in place. The risk register had included a high-impact, low-probability of industrial action at the client being a problem. Because it was thought to be a low probability, the only action taken was to provide a contractual solution that could be brought into play in such a situation – redefining costs and timetables. In fact, what actually happened was the blockade of petrol supply depots in protest at high prices/taxes. This was, in fact, handled reasonably because both parties agreed that there was nothing to be done, though the impact on the project certainly counted as a disaster. The delay in the roll-out meant that expensive support contracts had to be extended at short notice so that the old systems could be continued. However, it was clear that as the time approached, there might be such a problem; it was well documented in the media, so it could be argued that proper risk management could at least have identified better coping strategies. However, because the nature of the blockade was unpredictable – it might last days, weeks, or even months – there could have been no real contingency action that could have been taken to deal with the problem. Action could have been taken to mitigate some aspects, but the whole issue was beyond reasonable planning.

SUMMARY

Provided that the original project concept is correct, effective risk management will help reduce the chances of a disaster. For that reason alone, it is worth adopting best-practice risk-management processes. However, it cannot protect the project from the unknown, or from human error. Nor can it make a difference if the reality of the risks is not accepted – watering them down to make things look 'more acceptable' is a good way of starting on the path to disaster. No matter how much effort is put into risk management, there will still be project disasters. Some of the examples of project disasters given in this book used first-rate risk-management techniques, but it didn't save them. It is worth speculating how many more project disasters there would have been without risk management.

CHECKLIST

Answer the questions listed in Figure 4.3 for your project and take corrective action as needed. Where the answer is 'no', you need to do something about it. If you are dealing with a disaster, and don't understand the corrective action that will be required, get help from someone who does. You may not have time to learn the relevant skills yourself, but at least you now know the area of ignorance; this is step one to resolving the problem.

Question/comment	Yes/no?
Has a complete risk identification/assessment/planning exercise been conducted?	
Is there an 'owner' for this process?	
If not, have all the areas of risk been considered? As below: – commercial? – technical? – people? – political? – process? – change?	
For all the risks identified, is there a realistic assessment of impact and probability?	
Have these risks been ranked (prioritized) according to impact and probability?	

Figure 4.3 Checklist for corrective action

Question/comment	Yes/no?
For the higher-ranked risks, do suitable containment/ contingency/mitigation plans exist?	
Is the risk process being maintained/kept up to date?	
Are new risks being identified as the passage of time and change occurs?	
When new risks are identified are they being assessed/ prioritized along with the existing ones?	
Have both internal and external sources of risk been taken into account? Are risks being understated or ignored?	
What has changed?	
Where contingency/mitigation plans have been employed, is their effectiveness being monitored?	
Do all those involved understand the risk-management process?	
Are risks being actively minimized, as opposed to just being logged and observed?	
Is there management awareness of (and hopefully commitment to) the risk process?	

Figure 4.3 Checklist for corrective action (*continued*)

5

Human resources

The involvement of human resources (HR) in most project disasters is, sadly, often reduced to that of warning or sacking those who have been blamed for the disaster. This is a great shame as, firstly, it just panders to the blame culture, which doesn't help to solve the problem, and, secondly, HR can do so much more. In particular, one of the principal causes of project disasters described in Chapter 1 is resources – usually the lack of or the wrong resources. An effective HR department can really help here by reducing the load on the project manager who is trying to rescue the situation and by finding the right resource. It can also help with internal communications and support for the project team.

Note: HR (or personnel) departments vary in their remit, authority and capability considerably from one organization to the next. For this reason, and because the author is by no means an HR expert, this chapter restricts itself to areas where it is clear that HR can be of direct help to a project. It does not cover longer-term, or more career-specific and personal support-specific topics. Nor does it deal with HR processes/best practice.

WHAT IS HR FOR?

As already mentioned, HR (or personnel) functions have varying remits; however it is useful to get some sort of definition to set the scene. In his book on *HR Management Practice*, Michael Armstrong states that 'human resource management (HRM) aims to help the organization to achieve success through people.' He goes on to detail the key activities that an HRM function needs to deliver to support such an aim (see Figure 5.1). Those in *italics* are considered relevant to projects trying to survive a disaster. The quotation marks relate to text taken from Armstrong's book, sometimes edited for brevity.

Activity	Comment
Organization	'Organization design and development'. Where this encourages an open, flexible, cooperative culture, this can provide a good environment to help projects recover.
Employment relationship	'Improving the quality of the employment relationship by creating a climate of trust and by developing positive psychological contracts'. A common theme identified is that having a positive culture increases the chances of a good outcome.
Resourcing	'Human resource planning, talent management, recruitment and selection'. It is the last that is likely to be most relevant to helping out a project with problems.
Performance management	'Getting better results from the organization, teams and individuals by measuring and managing performance etc'. Not relevant to an imminent catastrophe,

Figure 5.1 HR and project disasters

Activity	Comment
	though it may be an indicator of future problems.
HR development	'Organizational and individual learning, management development, career management'. Only relevant in so far as they encourage a can-do, no-blame culture.
Reward management	'Pay schemes, contingent pay and non-financial rewards'. Again, not directly relevant other than as a background to the organization's culture.
Employee relations	'Industrial relations, employee voice, communications'. The communications aspect can be important.
Health and safety	'Making sure that the working environment meets requirements and protects employees from hazards and accidents as far as possible'. This can be essential if new or temporary working environments are being set up.
Welfare services	'Providing employees with individual services concerning such problems as prolonged illness, and services such as restaurants, etc'. Not directly relevant, though it can have a background cultural impact.
Employment and HR services	'Managing the employment relationship, administering HR policies and procedures and operating HR information systems'. Only important if they don't work as far as the project is concerned.

Figure 5.1 HR and project disasters (*continued*)

CULTURE

In Chapter 7, it is noted that the culture of an organization has a significant impact on its ability to react well to disasters and create the conditions for the best possible outcome. HR is well placed to affect the overall culture of an organization, and whilst this is not something that can be done overnight to help out a project, it is an area where HR can help in the longer term. Indeed, HR is better placed to affect the culture of an organization than most other functions, particularly where the organization is large or multi-national. In smaller organizations, the organization's founders often set the culture; here HR has less scope for change. Indeed, in many small-to-medium enterprises (SMEs), HR is little more than a hiring/firing and employment law compliance operation.

A limitation on the ability of HR to establish a culture that mitigates against project disasters and aids their recovery is the nature of the industry in which the organization operates. Manufacturing organizations tend to operate on ever-diminishing margins and have to be very lean, disciplined and efficient to survive. This tends to mean that a free and easy, very flexible cultural norm may not sit easily with the needs of the business. This does not mean, though, that a culture of honesty and openness cannot be fostered, and many manufacturing operations have shown that they benefit from this. However, as will be argued in Chapter 7 (Disaster and the organization) the best culture for project operations may not always be attainable.

Example: To foster creativity, 3M encourages its technical employees to spend up to 15 per cent of their time on projects of their own choosing. Also known as the 'bootlegging' policy, the 15 per cent rule has been the catalyst for some of 3M's most famous products, including Post-it™ Notes. A creative culture has been shown to be more likely to help turn a disaster around.

Note: Although it is suggested that a manufacturing organization may not be the best culture for dealing with a project disaster, this does not imply that manufacturing organizations are not good at projects!

RESOURCE SUPPORT

As mentioned in the introduction, the main area where HR can help a project in the throes of a disaster is with resources. This will usually require the rapid acquisition of appropriately skilled personnel, but may also involve reallocation of team members to other activities. There may also be more long-term resource issues to consider; it may well be the case that different staff are required to keep the project on track after it has been recovered. Similarly, those no longer needed will have to be found suitable opportunities if morale is to be maintained.

Key point: When dealing with a project manager or team that is experiencing a disaster, HR must take the impact of the disaster into account. There will probably be high stress levels, and rational thought may be at a premium. HR should offer support and not criticism and be prepared to act swiftly but not get caught up in any general panic.

Providing an outside view

Getting an outside view is a well-established component of many project-recovery strategies (see Chapters 8 and 9). HR can provide this by helping the project team review its resources against the requirements. They can also act as a non-involved assessor for any issues concerning the effectiveness, or otherwise, of project team members (including the project manager). They can provide an independent view of how the team is working and offer suggestions as to what would make it more effective.

In addition, because they are not part of the team in trouble, they are distanced from any personal issues that may have developed. They can take time to talk to people offline to establish whether there are things that bother them that they would not like to take up with a project or team manager. It may well be that a clash of personalities is significantly reducing productivity and trust within the team. It can be hard for those inside the team to do anything about this; they may not even recognize it. HR can provide a fair and reasonable assessment and should be able to offer support and guidance to resolve matters.

Suggestion: Where HR staff are not directly involved in resources for a project team, it can reduce pressure on the project manager and provide a healthy review to involve them. Where they are involved, they are of course already part of the team and will not be in a position to provide a sanity check.

Identifying resource requirements

This is an area where HR can take the load off the project team. They should be well equipped with the necessary expertise to establish what skills are needed, review those available in-house and have contacts with the outside world that allow them to outsource if required. They should also be able to identify the resource requirements by interviewing the project manger/specialist with a view to producing a job specification.

The project manager can help HR by thinking about the following points:

- What skills will they need?
- How long are they needed for?
- How many people are there with those skills and what utilization is needed (full/part time)?
- Whom they will report to?
- Will they have direct reports themselves?
- When are they needed from/to?
- Where will they be based?

Skills audits

In parallel with identifying what resources a project may need, HR may be able to provide a useful service in the form of a skills audit of the existing project team (and will often have a global view of skills available in the rest of the organization). This can be very useful in terms of identifying gaps, or more usefully for a project in trouble, identifying under-utilized talents. In a large project, it may well be the case that a gap in one project team that is causing major problems can be filled from another team – a skills audit will help identify this. HR can act as an in-house contract agency for sourcing specialist skills.

Temporary/contract resources

Where an additional, or different, resource is able to help improve the situation or prognosis for a troubled project, then it will invariably be needed quickly. For this reason, it will often be necessary to obtain the resource from the temporary or contract marketplace. Typically, this will be by way of an agency. In most organizations, it is the HR department that will, or should, have established relations with these agency suppliers of temporary labour. This is another area where HR can help. If a project manager goes to an agency directly, then they will need to spend a considerable amount of time producing the job specification, negotiating prices and margins and raising purchase orders and all the other things that go with such supply. This may well be something that the project manager has not done before, in which case it will certainly add to the administrative workload and may well take up a considerable amount of time at a point in the project when this is not to hand. HR should be expert in facilitating this, and this can only help the embattled project manager.

Permanent resources

Given that a project is in crisis, it is unlikely that an additional permanent resource can be recruited from the outside world in a sensible time frame to help matters. However, there may be people with the required skills in other parts of the organization who can be borrowed in the short term to help. It may be possible to swap out staff with the wrong skill set from the project team into more suitable areas. HR should have a skills profile for permanent members of staff and so should be able to match up any requirements with this relatively easily.

Example: Project X was in trouble; it really needed an expert SHF (super-high frequency) analogue designer to finish the design for a prototype piece of equipment needed to complete a technology demonstrator. Without the particular item, the organization would be eliminated from the competition to supply a high-value MoD contract. Time was at a premium, and there was certainly not enough time to go to the outside world to find a suitable recruit. Personnel (this was before it was called HR) were able to identify a suitable expert who was currently working on another MoD program (that had already been won) at a different site. It turned out to be possible to obtain this resource full-time for a couple of weeks without impacting the timetable for the other project. Knowing the skills available in the wider organization was all that was needed to solve the problem. In the organization in question at the time, with a strong engineering culture of self-dependence, it was unusual to involve personnel except for hiring and firing.

Note: HR must also be realistic in the expectation of the level of support that they can offer. Many modern, lean organizations have so little slack that there is no resource that can be begged or borrowed without damaging other functions too greatly.

Training

Where the right skills are not available within the team, the organization or via external recruitment, then training is an option that HR are likely to be able to help with. This extends to personal skills training as well – it may be possible to make a big change to a team's performance by suitable training. However, for a project that is already suffering a disaster, the time may not be practical to do this once the lead times and course availability have been taken into consideration. That said, there have been cases where taking a project team out for a facilitated team-building/brainstorming day has marked the turning point for a project. It is reasonable to ask HR for this kind of support.

Firing and hiring

Hopefully in organizations that have read this book and adopted its philosophy of avoiding blame at all costs, hiring and firing will not be part of the survival strategy for a project disaster. Sadly, the author's informal research has shown that people do get punished for their involvement in a project disaster, though this is sometimes not those who were actually responsible for it. More positively, new staff may be hired to help out with a project, though given the timetable for permanent staff recruitment this is unlikely to be done to provide an urgent fix to the problem. Where this has to happen, HR will need to be involved, but where the project is in a mess they are in a position to take the load off-line and help project managers by offering as much support as possible with this.

OTHER AREAS OF SUPPORT

These will vary considerably with the organization, the HR department and the individual project team, but the following spring to mind: stress, health and safety, and facilities.

Stress counselling/reduction

Although at the start of this book, is was clearly stated that 'it is not a book about psychological and trauma counselling', it is worth mentioning that HR can often point people in the right direction if they are suffering from stress. It is not altogether surprising that members of a project team that is in a tough situation may well be suffering from stress. Where this is the case, it makes sense to help them, as they will not be able to contribute as effectively as they might if they were not in a stressed state. (See also Appendix 2 on diagnosing if stress is an issue for a project team, and for a description as to what stress actually is – as opposed to healthy pressure.

Health and safety

Where temporary premises and equipment are being used, there are likely to be health and safety issues. The author remembers being put to work in a 'portakabin' that had been dumped in a car park. The electrical supply was made using a cable draped across the gap between an open window in the main building and a ventilation grill on the 'cabin', and the telephone line was tied to this cable with gaffer tape. Today, it is probable that such an arrangement would be illegal. Project disasters tend to call for ad hoc and short-term measures/short cuts that can cause more problems than they cure. HR can help here.

Facilities support

As well as helping with the supply of appropriate personnel, HR is often responsible for many of the services required by the workforce. This may be limited to the allocation of office space, but is more likely to include much more than this – typically, supply of telephone, connection to the IT infrastructure (via the IT department), health and safety, computer rooms, electrical power, security staff, air conditioning, office furniture and so forth.

Example: The resolution of one disaster, where the system required connection of a sales-collection system to the back-office billing and charging system, did not work on time and was to employ many temporary staff to rekey the information. These relatively unskilled temporary staff had to be obtained at short notice, and more importantly, they had to be housed. The HR department involved had to find the physical space at short notice and had to ensure that necessary desks and chairs, with appropriate services (power, light, communications and so forth) were available. They also had to work in conjunction with the IT department to make sure that the right terminals, network connections and software was available. On top of this was the need to ensure that health and safety regulations were met, to ensure that there was appropriate training for the temporary workers and to negotiate a decent price with the agency. They also became involved in interviewing the temporary staff. HR can be a major contributor to a disaster recovery.

COMMUNICATIONS

Another area where HR can help is in internal communications where it is easy for serious damage to be done if matters are not handled well. A common form of fallout from a project disaster is the wildfire spread of rumour. Rumours may be made worse because of the 'Chinese-whispers' effect.

Example: Chinese-whispers effect

Project X for a leading European manufacturer was in considerable trouble: a critical deadline for equipment delivery was missed which meant that the service to the client would be delayed by a few days. The contracted service date was 27 July. The delay caused this to slip until 4 August. In reality, this was not a disaster, but the client was annoyed and had pointed out that there were penalty clauses for late delivery. In fact, the delay of a few days was not an issue, but the information evolved as follows. 1. 'We've missed a deadline, the delivery has slipped into next month, there has been talk of penalty clauses.' 2. 'They're a month late and it is going to cost us.' 3. 'Project X is in a mess, they're over a month late and the client is going to take the company to the cleaners.' Admittedly, this example is exaggerated to make a point, but this is what can happen.

HR can be well placed to nip this type of situation, which can make a problem seem like a disaster, in the bud. If they are made aware of an issue, then they are in a position to communicate what is really happening. In the case of the above example, a short e-mail would be appropriate along the lines of 'Although Project X has suffered a delay, the team are working with the client to resolve the problem, and both sides are confident of a positive outcome. There is no question of penalty charges being levied, and a revised delivery schedule has been agreed.' Ideally, this type of communication needs to be made before rumours have got out of hand, or it can be seen as a propaganda exercise and can lead to yet more rumours, 'what are they trying to hide?' It is a judgement call to decide when to involve HR for such a purpose; only when a serious project event has occurred should it be needed. (See also Chapter 6, on PR, for additional information on internal and external communications.)

SUMMARY

HR can be helpful in supporting a project team when there is a disaster; they should not be thought of merely as a hiring and firing facility. They can help with surviving the disaster by taking some of the load off the project team with resource and facilities issues, thus freeing-up time to actually retrieve the situation. They should not be seen as the last port of call for a drowning project manager, but rather should be involved early. HR can also help develop the type of culture (open, honest, non-blaming, flexible and so forth) that will help avoid a disaster in the first place and provide the best working environment to recover from one once it has started.

CHECKLIST

Answer the HR-related questions listed in Figure 5.2 for your project and take corrective action as needed. If you are dealing with a disaster and don't understand the corrective action that will be required, get help from someone who does. You may not have time to learn the relevant skills yourself, but at least you now know the area of ignorance; this is step one to resolving the problem.

Question/comment	Yes/no?
Do you know what support services your organization's HR function can provide?	
For example: – training? – health and safety advice? – interviewing and assessment? – welfare services? – internal (organization) communications facilities? – skills audits? – recruitment?	
So you have skills issues?	
Are your 'people' resources as needed? Too little/wrong resource?	
Is there a health and safety issue?	
Is the team suffering from stress so much that it affects the way they work? Can HR offer support in this area?	
Does the project need to communicate with the rest of the company?	
Can HR help provide an outside view of the problem?	
Can HR provide information about skills and experience available elsewhere in the organization?	
Are additional facilities needed to support the project?	
Do employees need to be hired/fired or formally disciplined?	
Are HR able to assist with motivation/reward issues needed to help the project recover?	

Figure 5.2 HR checklist

6

Public relations

Some project managers consider that the last thing they want to become involved in during a project disaster is public relations (PR). There will be some who wouldn't even expect there to be any mention of it in a book on project disasters. However, the fact that a project is a disaster makes ignoring PR difficult; also the related skills are often at the low end of the average project manager's portfolio. Consequently, the PR world deserves a little more detail than has been given to other skills areas, for example risk management, where the reader is more likely to have a solid understanding of what is involved.

Disasters tend to focus the minds of the public relations fraternity, if not drive them into a frenzy of activity. DABGA is an acronym well known in the psychological world; it stands for **D**enial, **A**nger, **B**argaining, **G**rief and **A**cceptance. In the PR world, the traditional approach to a project disaster is DA. By default, they will **D**eny that any disaster has occurred and be **A**ngry that anyone has suggested that it might have happened. This is not a reaction limited to those in the PR business; many marketing and senior management people seem to follow the same path. As with HR, this really undersells what can actually be done with PR to help survive the impact of a disaster. There are two areas where PR needs to be considered; the more obvious one is external, the other is internal. Both are important, but the internal aspects seem to be most often ignored. This is always a mistake, and this chapter will show how both elements can help the project to survive the aftermath of a disaster.

A classic example of denial took place on BBC Radio 4's 'Today' programme. The item was following up a report from an eight-month probe by MPs into government computer systems that had found an 'appalling waste of public money'. Singling out a specific agency for particular criticism, the MPs said the agency's phone and computer system was 'over-spec, over-budget and overdue'. The committee said there should be a full 'post-mortem' into the installation of the agency's computer system so lessons could be learned.

Development costs had risen from £200M to £456M, and the system went live after a 2-year delay. However, even then, the system did not work satisfactorily, and MPs suggested that it should be cancelled if it did not work correctly 'very soon'. The changes needed to the system were expected to further increase costs.

The interview was between the presenter and the spokesman for the company that was responsible for the project. It is necessary to understand that the project was carried out under what is known as PFI (private finance initiative). Under this system, the Government pays for the service, typically on a per-transaction, usage basis. The Government does not pay directly for the development costs. The interview went something like this (it has been edited for brevity and to emphasize the point; and is not a true and accurate record).

Interviewer 'How much over-budget is the project and when will it be delivered?'
Company man 'Let's step back and consider what the system was like before this – paper-based, complicated and full of delays – a very messy system. We've replaced it with a system that can deal

with the process based on just a single phone call – a much better solution that improves the service to the public.' (This went on in a similar vein for quite a while.)

Interviewer 'To get back to the question, how much over-budget is the project and when will it be delivered compared to the original date?'

Company man 'This is a PFI project.'

Interviewer 'Can you answer the question?'

Company man 'I am answering the question; the development is paid for by the company, the Government just pays for the service. If we don't deliver the service, we don't get paid.'

Interviewer 'How much over-budget?'

Company man 'The Government is not paying for any of the development.'

Interviewer 'So the Government is not having to pay anything more for the service?'

Company man 'It is paying more than originally expected because the systems were more complex than originally envisaged.'

Interviewer 'So it is going to cost more. MPs say that if it isn't working properly soon, then it should be scrapped; when will it be working?'

Company man 'We will deliver a robust and effective service by the end of the year.'

Interviewer 'It is already very late, and a House of Commons committee has suggested that if it does not work soon it should be cancelled.'

Company man 'As I said, it is important to deliver a robust and effective system, which we will do by the end of the year.'

The sad fact is that although the company man stonewalled very effectively, the listener was left in no doubt that the project was a mess and that the tax payer would end up footing the bill in terms of higher service charges. The strategy of denial did not enhance the company's reputation, nor did it fool anyone into thinking that there were no problems. It might have been better to take a more cooperative and open approach.

WHAT DOES PR DO ANYWAY?

PR is a much-maligned term, synonymous in many people's minds with the sins of the spin-doctor. However, the reality is more positive: PR is the business of communicating with the outside world. However, as PR has now been extended to include internal communications within many organizations, it can be simplified to the business of communication.

Overall, PR can be expected to cover image, publicity and the dissemination of information (see Figure 6.1).

Role	Description
Image	In many cases, image is the major role played by PR. It is all too easy for the outside world to have a negative image of an organization. This may well be based on misconceptions because the correct information has not been communicated well. In the case of an organization which is experiencing a high-profile project disaster, then effective PR is needed to protect the corporate profile.
Publicity	Here PR works to get more and more publicity for an organization or individual to raise the profile. This usually involves getting as much media coverage as possible.
Information	PR can play a major role in communicating information to the intended (and often a wider) audience in a factual and easily digested format, the goal being to overcome the audience's ignorance.

Figure 6.1 Typical role of PR

EXTERNAL PR

Most organizations have some function that fulfils the role of PR. This may be a specific PR department, an external agency, or a part of the sales or marketing department. They are unlikely to be involved in a project disaster until after it has become public knowledge – by which time is almost always too late. The following example is based upon a composite of several project disasters recounted to the author/reported in the press.

Example: In this case, Company B was responsible for implementing a change to an air-traffic control system. For reasons that do not concern us, there was a chance it might fail – it did, with no impact on safety, but it resulted in the best part of a day's delay in flights over a reasonably wide area. The publicity in the aftermath was damning for both the client and Company B. Nothing had been prepared, and the media had them consistently on the back foot, scrambling to answer questions. It is not being suggested that PR would have made any difference to the impact of the failed project, but if a communication strategy had been in place beforehand, things would have been better. Informed parties would have been able to apologize and to explain what had been done, why it had been a reasonable strategy, and what was being done to rectify the problem.

It is usually a more successful strategy to get whoever is responsible for PR involved as early as possible. It would seem to be good practice to include PR in the briefing for any projects that might have the capacity to embarrass the organization.

Key point: Involve any PR function as soon as you become aware that something may go badly wrong. Asking them to clear up the mess once you have said something stupid to the press is not going to work.

Media

An example of how the media can be seen as hostile to a project, even becoming a cause of a disaster before there is one, is the multi-billion pound NHS IT project (history will have told how this project has fared by the time this book is published). Richard Grainger, NHS IT Chief, speaking at a London summit in May 2004, attacked the media questioning of the project as scaremongering and asked for 'space to get on successfully with what we have been doing for the last 18 months'. He clearly viewed coverage as a threat to the project. Later in the same conference, during a panel session, senior team members were asked about their major concerns, and identified sheer magnitude, need for clinician buy-in, and the importance of local leadership to carry through implementation of the centrally delivered system. They did not list press coverage as a cause for concern. (Source: *Computer Weekly*, 18 May 2004.)

At the time of writing, this project is still attracting considerable publicity – on 12 October 2004, a lead story on the BBC pertained to its budget: 'officials at the Department of Health had estimated the total costs of the programme at between £18.6bn and £31bn. The declared cost was £6.2bn.'

Press releases

For the higher-profile disaster, another channel of communication will be the press release. Most sizeable organizations will have a press office, employing people whose job it is to deal with press releases, including writing and distribution. A press release needs to include:

- when it is to be released;
- who wrote/authorized it;
- who to refer questions to;
- the actual information that needs to be released.

Communications strategy

Once a project disaster gets into the realm of the outside world, it is vital to have a communications strategy; like him or loathe him, this was one of Alastair Campbell's major strengths. He and his team managed the media throughout any crisis by having a detailed chart saying who was going to say what, to whom, when and where. It is not suggested that this is the approach that needs to be taken for the average project disaster. However, a simple strategy can help get the message across (whatever that happens to be) and can save wasting considerable amounts of time.

Key point: Have a strategy before rather than after events get out of hand.

INTERNAL PR

Although this is often ignored by those working on PR (irrespective of the job title of the people performing the role), who tend to concentrate on what the outside world thinks, the benefits of internal PR can be considerable. As with the external case, the sooner PR function is involved the better – it is hard for them to do any good once rumour and miscommunication have done their work.

The following scenario is offered as an example of what can happen without the benefit of effective internal PR/communication.

Example: Project X was in a total mess. All tasks on the critical path were late, the equipment supplier had gone bankrupt, and essential equipment had not been shipped. The project team was demoralized, and the project manager considered that her job was under threat. The project was to deliver a significant upgrade to the organization's IT infrastructure that affected every member of the organization's ability to access e-mail or the internet. There was no official communications strategy associated with the project, so the main means of distributing the bad news was by rumour, and therefore was both uncontrolled and often inaccurate. Typical of the rumours going the rounds were 'The systems will completely crash or be inoperable!'

However, where PR is used effectively to help the project team, a positive contribution can be made.

Communications strategy

While perhaps not as critical as it is in surviving contact with the outside world, having a communications strategy for the project team when dealing with the rest of the organization can be very helpful. As for the outside world, it comes down to agreeing who is going to say what to whom, and when. It can be very time-wasting if the project team has to spend too much duplicated effort on explaining the nature of the problem to uncoordinated interested parties.

GIVING BAD NEWS

The secret here is to state openly what is happening and what is being done to counter the problems. Hiding bad news or attempting to brush the complexity of the problems under the carpet will lead to mistrust and disbelief (see also Chapter 9).

HANDLING QUESTIONS

This is a crucial session skill. No matter how well you have handled the problems, if you handle questions badly you will undo all the good that you have done. Handling questions takes considerable discipline. Here is a technique that allows you to stay in control and handle questions effectively. We call it the STOP technique.

First you need to listen to the question all the way through and then, before you answer:

- **S** Share the question (where appropriate) with the rest of the audience, who won't have heard it because they were all too busy thinking about the questions they wanted to ask.
- **T** Think about how you are going to answer the question.

- **O** Only answer the question – don't get side-tracked and don't go into too much detail.
- **P** Politely check that your answer was OK.

SURVIVING THE MEDIA

If a project disaster is sufficiently high profile to require explanations and information release to the outside world, then it has to be done well. The obvious stonewalling and obfuscation given in the example at the beginning of this chapter is not the way to do it. Keep in mind that it is only the most significant project disasters that are likely to be newsworthy. The following advice covers what you need to do before spending five minutes of infamy before the media. It is hard to make the ratio of preparation and planning time to interview time too high. If all this seems to be daunting, particularly when dealing with national radio/ TV, then it is time to think about getting a professional spokesperson to help.

Stage 1: Pre-interview research

Careful thought and preparation is always needed before you speak to the media. Not being fully briefed on all aspects of the situation and not being in possession of the real facts is dangerous. Particularly when dealing with the national media, you can be sure that they will have done extensive research. If the media know something that the interviewee does not, then trouble is close at hand. This pre-interview research needs to be done as thoroughly as possible; sitting down and writing a press release and a crib sheet is not enough.

Why are you talking to the media anyway?

As shown in Figure 6.2, the reasons for talking to the media vary according to whether you are a spokesperson, expert, trouble-shooter or involved party.

Role	Description
Spokesperson	Someone speaking on behalf of the organization, but not necessarily directly involved in the disaster/project. Such a person would be expected to have a specific brief and not be expected to answer any/all questions off-the-cuff.
Expert	Expert in the subject matter that relates to the disaster. The remit is the area of expertise. If the interviewee is an employee of the organization, then this must be made clear; no impression of independence should be given. An independent expert is usually seen as more credible. The expert is there to explain the problem/solution from a technical point of view.
Troubleshooter	Someone brought in to sort out the disaster (either from within the organization or from outside). They will be putting across the solution to the problem, stressing positive outcomes.
Involved party	A member of the project or management team, there because of inside knowledge and the ability to put forward an informed view.

Figure 6.2 Reasons for talking to the media

Why is the media talking to you, and what are they looking for?

As shown in Figure 6.3, there are a variety of reasons as to why the media would wish to talk to you, and these revolve essentially around whether they want a quote, a victim, an explanation, a political statement, an advertisement or input from an expert.

Why/what	Description
A quote	Essentially a 'sound bite' or an eye-witness account of what is going on. This is one of the easier experiences – as long as the interviewee gets it right. It is very easy to make an off-the-cuff remark that will cause all hell to break loose. Encourage the interviewee to engage brain before opening mouth.
A victim	Here they will be trying to get the interviewee to accept fault themselves, for their organization, or to get the blame placed on a third party. It is assumed that you are part of the organization that owns the project that is going wrong. Consequently, the advice that is given above – think before speaking – goes double.
An explanation	They are seeking the cause of what went wrong and why. They will be trying to attribute blame if at all possible.
A political statement	If your role is a political one, perhaps a local or national-level politician, civil servant, or you are managing a project on behalf of such a person, you may have to make a political statement. However, this is outside the scope of this book and you are on your own here.
An advertisement	Unlikely in the case of a project disaster, though if things are being quickly turned around there may be an opportunity here.
Input from an expert	In this role, you are there because of your specific expertise. For example, if it is a civil engineering disaster, you may be an expert on stressed structures. You will either be independent or an expert from within the project team. This book assumes you are in the latter category.

Figure 6.3 Reasons for the media talking to you

What do they want to talk about?

There are a number of standard topics that the media will want to interview you about, and they include: the company, the company's actions, the company's views on a subject, a news item, you, your job or your expertise. However, in this case, they will want to interview you about the current disaster, and the aspect of the disaster will depend largely upon your role in the project.

What limits do you need to put on what you say?

Limits as to what will be discussed need to be determined before any interview takes place, and will need to be agreed with the interviewer(s) in advance (Figure 6.4). This is common practice for political interviews (politicians do not like to be ambushed with questions they are not prepared for), and will not raise eyebrows.

Limit	Description
What subjects are you prepared to talk about?	Make a list of what it is you want to talk about. For example, you may wish to talk about what is going to be done next to fix the problem, the timetable and commitment to the solution, and why it is the best solution. This should include any main points you wish to get across.
What subjects are off-limits?	Just as important is to define what will not be discussed, even if this means resorting to the traditional 'no comment'. For example, it may not be acceptable to say how much money the organization has lost at this stage, or, if the cause of the problem is not fully diagnosed, you may not wish to enter into speculation that might prove to be wrong in the future.
What legal aspects are involved?	It is important to have a basic grasp of what can get you or the organization into legal difficulties. In essence, this boils down to telling lies or

Figure 6.4 Imposing limits on what will be discussed in the interview

Limit	Description
	slandering (or, if it is to be printed, libelling) someone. Get advice if possible; if this is not possible, then think before speaking and avoid making accusations or denigrating anyone or any organization – however strongly you feel about the matter. It is not enough to know something is true; if you cannot prove it, then the legal profession will be set to gather more fees.
Do you know the company line on the subject?	Knowing the company line on a subject can be important, at least in terms of career progress, and you should investigate this carefully if you have the time. Any organization that fails to provide a briefing is asking for trouble, but it will be the interviewee that gets the blame for getting it wrong.
How can you deflect questions if necessary?	There are many techniques available for dealing with hostile or difficult interview questions. If you are not already familiar with these techniques, then it is a good idea to obtain some training (for a price, this can be obtained very quickly) or consider using a spokesperson who does. For those who are really dropped in it, then see the survival hints in Stage 3 of this section.

Figure 6.4 Imposing limits on what will be discussed in the interview (*continued*)

Where will the interview take place?

As shown in Figure 6.5, the decision as to where the interview will take place is an important one.

Which media?

None of the media will be an easy ride, but some have the potential to be much tougher than others (Figure 6.6).

Golden rule: Treat all microphones as live. The late President Regan probably made the most famous example of this blunder when he said, in 1984, at the height of the Cold War: 'My fellow

Location	Features
In your office	You are on home ground and are therefore more likely to be relaxed. By comparison, the interviewer will not be; this is a good situation to be in. Furthermore, you will have additional information to hand and access to colleagues if needed.
Over the telephone	Being interviewed over the telephone can be tricky as you will be at the mercy of uncertain communications technology and, worse, get no visual feedback from the interviewer or the audience.
At their offices	Not your territory, so you are at a disadvantage. However, it is reasonable to assume that the office environment is a familiar one, so it should not be too threatening.
At their studios	Unless you are in the media business, then this will be an alien world. It is not an environment that is familiar, and it is not home ground.
Neutral ground	Neutral ground provides a level playing field, but leaves you in the position of having access only to what you have in you head, or in whatever supporting notes you have with you.

Figure 6.5 Deciding on the location of the interview

Americans, I am pleased to tell you I just signed legislation which outlaws Russia forever. The bombing begins in five minutes.' He thought the microphone was off. It was transmitted worldwide. The same goes for cameras.

Other key questions

As detailed in Figure 6.7, there are a number of other important questions that need to be resolved before the interview takes place.

Media	Description
Local radio	This is likely only if the project disaster has some local significance. For example, a civil engineering project may have a severe impact on local traffic if something goes badly wrong. There is a considerable range in the approach of local radio, and the interviewers may well be fairly pushy if they are using local radio as their stepping stone. Prepare as if for national radio. Such interviews may be live or taken off-line and then edited prior to transmission. Being live tends to be more stressful, though it is easier to be caught off-guard when doing the off-line kind. Remember that any microphone should be considered a live one. If possible, get the right to hear the edited version, and if necessary withdraw it, prior to transmission. Editing can completely change the impression that the interview makes.
Local newspaper	Again, likely where there is significant local impact. As with local radio, do not assume a smooth ride; the interviewer may well be out for a 'story' rather than sober reporting of the facts. These interviews will not be 'live'.
Trade press	Probably the easiest ride, though not always if the journal has a particular bee in its bonnet, for example about public-sector project failures. Usually people familiar with your business and its problems will conduct these interviews. The standard of professionalism does vary somewhat from sector to sector, and the calibre of the reporter will depend on the significance of the disaster. By and large, trade publications tend to be kinder as they depend on the organizations they are reporting for advertising revenue, but don't rely on this instead of preparing properly.

Figure 6.6 Deciding on which media to use

Media	Description
National magazines	Magazine feature writers do not usually interview people in the midst of a project disaster; they tend to take a longer and more complete view.
National radio	One of the most challenging; if this is in doubt listen to John Humphrys interviewing on BBC Radio 4's 'Today' programme. The interviewer may not be expert in your subject area but will be very well briefed and will be expert in all the techniques of interviewing and pressing home a point. The best defence for the non-professional interviewee (such as a politician) is to tell the truth simply and clearly and not to get angry under any circumstances. Remember that the microphone is always live.
National press	This is serious; for a project disaster to merit attention from the likes of the 'broadsheets' means it is of national interest. It is vital to have a professional approach to this, ideally with professional help. In the unlikely event that a 'red top' is interested, then there is either some form of scandal involved or it is political with a capital 'P'.
Local television	This is high-profile coverage; even local television in the UK has audience figures in the hundreds of thousands to million bracket. As with radio, keep in mind that the microphone should always be treated as 'on' – the same goes for the camera.
National television	After national radio, national television is likely to be the toughest test for anyone. In particular, if it is live, then it is likely to be very stressful for the inexperienced. Always start from the premise that the interviewer is on home ground and you are in an alien environment with bright, hot lights, and distracting things happening all around you; what is more, you will be under time pressure if it is live. Do not enter into this lightly.

Figure 6.6 Deciding on which media to use (*continued*)

Who will be interviewing you?	This is more critical for the higher-profile media. At least you can get to hear/see them in action before you meet them – something they won't have had the chance to do with you.
How long will it take?	This is critical; if there is a fixed time limit, then you need to know this to get any key points across early (particularly if 'live'). It can also help if you need to avoid answering a particular question (though note the warning given at the beginning of this chapter; it is easy to detect playing for time/stonewalling). A typical national radio or television news interview will vary from about 30 seconds to a couple of minutes (unless you are the Prime Minister, in which case they may want you for rather longer). A newspaper interview or one for a feature programme may be in the range 15–45 minutes. In the case of obtaining information for this book, the longest interview was just over an hour.
What power of veto do you have?	If the interview is not live, it may be possible to have some sort of editorial right (usually negotiated in return for granting the interview) after the event. This needs to be agreed in advance, though keep in mind that journalists write their own story; only when someone, or a fact, is quoted will they have a duty to get it right. In practice, they can put any interpretation they wish on the facts/quotes. Not for nothing is the journalist's motto 'make it short, make it snappy, make it up!'
Will you need an expert on hand?	This will not be practical for a live interview, though you may wish to have someone available to give you a last-minute briefing. However, for other interviews, it may well be helpful to have suitable experts on hand, perhaps including a legal expert to refer to 'offline'.

Figure 6.7 Other important questions

| What do you want to say? | It is as well to have an agenda before starting any interview. What points should be made, what supports any case that is to be put forward? This should not be done in isolation and should involve the team. The person giving the interview needs to check assumptions with the people who are actually involved at the detail level if errors of fact are to be avoided. |

Figure 6.7 Other important questions (*continued*)

Where to find help before the interview

As presented in Figure 6.8, there are two important sources from which help can be obtained before the interview – HR and PR/marketing.

| HR | They should be able to get you training and to help you find a spokesperson. |
| PR/marketing | As above – it will depend on the organization and its structure. |

Figure 6.8 Where to find help

Stage 2: Preparing yourself for the interview

Getting ready for the interview involves preparing yourself, particularly preparing what you want to say (Figure 6.9).

Stage 3: The interview

Technique

As detailed in Figure 6.10, there are a number of interview techniques that should be practised before the interview itself.

Item	Notes
First impressions 1: What to wear	First impressions count. If you don't believe this, get hold of a tape of the Nixon/Kennedy interview from the 1960s. Although verbally Nixon did well, his five o'clock shadow and sallow, un-made-up complexion made all viewers give the prize to the appealing looking Kennedy.
First impressions 2: Warming up your voice	If you are going to talk to a large audience and need to project your voice, you should make an effort to warm your voice up before you speak to the audience. A dry throat, nerves and strain make it very likely that your first words will cause you to cough. On the way to the interview, recite nursery rhymes or rehearse some of your statements aloud. Whisper them forcibly and then chant them loudly. This warms and loosens up the vocal cords.
Working from notes/scripts	In an interview, as opposed to a presentation, it is unlikely that you will be able to follow a script. However, structured notes covering salient points are helpful. Consider using Mind Maps™ or simply a series of headings with useful information under each one. Make sure the notes are easy to use, and easy to read (apply the glance test – if you can't read what is under a heading at a single glance, then it is unlikely that it will be of much use in a live interview). Notes can be more elaborate and detailed for non-live interviews, where it is reasonable to ask for time to look things up.
Rehearsal	Assuming there is time, a rehearsal is most helpful. The best way to do this for an interview is for somebody to role-play the part of the interviewer.

Figure 6.9 Preparing yourself for the interview

Item	Notes
Handouts/press statements	Handouts/press statements can be useful, particularly where you have not been able to get all the points across because of time or interviewer intervention. They have the significant benefit of being entirely within the organization's control. (See earlier subsection detailing what might be useful in a press release and its structure.)

Figure 6.9 Preparing yourself for the interview (*continued*)

Issue	Recipe for success
Handling nerves	Slow yourself down and breathe slowly.
Keeping cool during an interview	Don't rush to answer. Listen to the questions all the way through. Stick, as far as is possible, to your plan.
Speed, pause and emphasis	The more nervous you are, the more likely you are to gabble. One way to slow your speech down is to make sure that you articulate the ends of your words clearly.
Body language and credibility	Keep the eye contact high, straighten your back and keep your hands above your waist if possible.
Gaining thinking time	Repeat the question or ask the questioner what it is they want to know. Pauses in your own speech will seem extremely long to you – they are never actually as long as they seem.
Handling difficult questions	These are the ones you should have thought about before the session. Don't treat all questions as if they are hostile. Keep your answers short and to the point.
Deflecting, deferring, defusing and dismissing	There is no rule that says you have to answer every single question. Specialist questions that only interest one member of the audience should be taken off-line.

Figure 6.10 Interview technique

Stage 4: Post-interview

Following up the interview

After the event, it is as well to take stock; unless your disaster is well under control, there will almost certainly be more interest. Keep in mind that the media all keep an eye on one another for a good story.

Debriefing your team

Most important of all for the project manager or team member who has been through the media mill is to update the team. If possible, do this before talking to senior management/marketing/ HR, etc, though this will not always be possible. If the interview was live, then the team may well have heard it when it went out. However, they may well not know what the thinking was behind the answers given. Ideally, you will have consulted the project team before giving the interview, so there should be few surprises, barring accidents.

A POSITIVE EXAMPLE

The following is from an interview with Professor Pillinger (copied from the BBC website http://news.bbc.co.uk/1/hi/sci/tech/3926253.stm):

PP 'Whenever people argued that Beagle didn't have mobility, I would argue it did. We were going to go down instead of across. I think down is a very important place to go [on Mars],' he told delegates at the conference. Professor Pillinger was referring to the 'mole', a burrowing instrument designed to obtain a soil sample from beneath the surface. The Open University professor also mused on the factors that might have scuppered his first attempt to land on the Red Planet.'

PP 'We don't know what went wrong. It could have been something as simple as a tiny resistor in a communications chain.'

PP 'Our best bet is that the gremlins of Mars changed the composition of the atmosphere to the point where it was thinner than we anticipated so we didn't make it to the surface.' But he added: 'I should remind you that Beagle 2 was named after the ship HMS Beagle that took Charles Darwin around the world. It was the second voyage of HMS Beagle which was the important one, not the first.'

This final quote linking a follow-up Beagle mission with the second voyage of Darwin's ship shows how a first-rate analogy can be built into a short quote – it is more than a mere sound bite.

SUMMARY

Project disasters can rarely, if ever, be kept within the project team and the sponsoring organization. If the news escapes by rumour and third-hand reporting, then human nature will ensure that the situation will be presented as being even worse than it actually is. 'They don't know what they're doing, they are like headless chickens, Smith is for the chop', and so on. Also, where the media are involved, they will have an agenda of news-making as well as reporting, which will rarely do anything to help the case. If things are not handled well, more effort will be spent in dealing with the thirst for information of the world outside the project than in trying to get things sorted out. Consequently, having the right approach to PR can be vital in giving a project a chance to make any kind of recovery. Once matters have descended into open warfare, the blame game will assert itself and all will be lost.

CHECKLIST

Answer the PR-related questions for your project presented in Figure 6.11 and take corrective action as needed. If you are dealing with a disaster and don't understand the corrective action that will be required, get help from someone who does. You may not have time to learn the relevant skills yourself, but at least you now know the area of ignorance; this is step one to resolving the problem.

Question/comment	Yes/no
Do I know all the facts?	
How much does the company/team/outside world need to know?	
What are their greatest concerns?	
How can we work towards a solution?	
Can the PR department help? Does the project need help relating to: – image? – publicity? – information/communication (internal and/or external)?	
Do you need to interact with the media? If so, which of these, and are you comfortable with them? – local radio? – local/trade press? – national press? – national radio? – local/national TV?	
Has a communications strategy been developed?	
Has 'DABGA' been taken into account?	
If you are to be interviewed, have you prepared for it by: – researching? – rehearsing? – identifying your role? – identifying your goals? – identifying your power of veto/level of control?	
After any interviews, have you debriefed: – your team? – your management/advisers?	

Figure 6.11 Checklist: Making the most of PR

7

Disaster and the organization

Project disasters do not exist in a vacuum; they exist within an organization and, ultimately, the outside world. Those working on a project that has become a disaster will tend to be very focused on their own world, often to the exclusion of anything else. This is something that needs to be fought against, as salvation may well only be available with help from external sources. Similarly, it is not unknown for some organizations to ignore project disasters for fear of guilt by association, or a simple desire to pretend it isn't happening. This is not a good idea either; project disasters can have a significant impact on the whole organization if not managed properly. Getting the best outcome from a project disaster is more likely if the project team and the organization work together.

Before this can happen effectively, the project and the organization have to have an understanding of how one affects the other.

HOW THE ORGANIZATION AFFECTS THE PROJECT

The organization is the environment in which the project exists, and its response to a disaster will speak volumes about its culture. That culture will also have a significant effect on how the disaster evolves and its subsequent outcome. The areas where the organization impacts the project include: culture, support, flexibility and finance (Figure 7.1).

Feature	Commentary
Culture	This is a slightly abstract property of an organization (see example) and there are many definitions concerning it. Properties that go to make up an organization's culture include: open or secretive, hierarchical, team-based, communication norms, political, customer driven, sales driven, product or service oriented, process driven, ad-hoc, creative, employee development, staff turnover (churn), short or long term, etc; there are others, but they are all of a similar type. They give clues as to how the organization will react to a given situation – in some cases, different parts of an organization have different cultures. Some aspects of their culture are subject to external forces; for instance, in publicly quoted companies, shareholder pressure for short-term results can be the root of longer-term problems. Companies that have a heavy 'blame' culture seem both more prone to disasters and find it harder to recover from them.
Support	The support structures available within an organization, such as facilities, human resources, information technology, public relations, quality assurance and so on, make a difference. Simply put, the more support centres are available to the project, the better the chances of getting help to recover from the problem(s) at hand. Being able to draw upon external expertise significantly improves the chances of recovering from a bad situation. The more

Figure 7.1 How the organization affects the project

Feature	Commentary
	knowledge and experience there is to draw upon, the more hope there is of finding a solution. The caveat on this is how easy or difficult it is to make use of this expertise — the level and effectiveness of management support is important here.
Flexibility	In organizations that have very rigid operating processes, it can be difficult to make rapid changes. Given that a project is in trouble, it is likely that things will need doing fast if recovery is to be effected. Flexibility also impacts the ability to, for example, swap staff between operating units to fix a skills crisis. Similarly, the ability to set up new office space quickly to accommodate additional staff, either in the short or long term, can be important. The downside of this is that many lean organizations simply cannot afford to carry the overhead that such flexibility implies. A consequence of this is that manufacturing-oriented organizations (which have to be lean to survive) tend to find project working more of a potential problem than service organizations. Fast moving and flexible organizations have a better chance of recovering from a disaster — an organization that cannot deliver this should consider outsourcing project work to organizations that can.
Finance	Once a project has got to the disaster stage, there is usually a budget issue. In many cases, it was underestimating the budget in the first place that caused the problem. A project that is running on time, with no problems, will typically be not too far off its budget. One that is behind and possibly out of control may not even know what has been spent! The financial status of the organization will be a significant parameter in determining what can be done to help a project. At the crudest level, if the organization is in difficulty itself, then it is unlikely to be able to supply the project with additional funding. Having a substantial bankroll available to bail out a failing project can avert, or enable recovery from, a disaster. However, the desire to avoid failure should not be used to support a bad business case. Deep pockets should always be allied to sound financial controls — organizations with sound financial control are better suited to disaster avoidance and recovery.

Figure 7.1 How the organization affects the project (*continued*)

Example (culture): One customer of the author's was a US parent company with a substantial European operation. The cultures of the European arm contrasted markedly with the somewhat 'red neck' elements of the parent company, but this usually only became a problem where joint teams were set up between the US and European organizations. The author still relishes a story from a similar mixed environment, where the US staff could not believe it when employees (of a customer) at a meeting in Norway simply got up and went home because it was going home time. A year later, the US folk were still talking about it; sadly the advice 'when in Rome. . .' seemed to have passed them by. Maybe they should also wonder whether Norwegians live longer!

What cultures encourage the best outcomes?. . .

There is a consensus among many management experts that the organizational culture that provides the most helpful environment for recovering from disasters is an open one. A culture where information is shared, problems are seen as being there to be overcome, and where clients are actively involved in progress gives the best chance of fixing things. It also gives the best chance of avoiding the disasters in the first place. Unsurprisingly, an environment where the decisions are taken by those with the knowledge and experience to make them is also helpful.

Example: An example of an organization that adopted a positive approach was (and hopefully still is) the General Electric Company, whose CEO (John Welsh, CEO 1981–2001) had a refreshingly positive approach to projects that failed. He took the view that project disasters/failures should not automatically result in career-damaging outcomes. He felt that to do so would prevent anyone taking risks with new ideas and leading-edge opportunities. The view was that one bold success could outweigh the effect of many failures, but this is not to say that the idea was to encourage bad practice, poor procedures and so forth. Rather, the goal was to create a culture in which project managers could take on a project and then feel safe to shut it down if it looked like becoming a disaster. Many organizations continue to run projects long after they should have been abandoned because the price of failure for those involved is seen as being too high.

Example: No disaster was involved in this instance. The author was fortunate enough to be taken around the Benetton (now Renault) Formula 1 factory. It was particularly interesting to note that all the engineering IT design and support systems were open to inspection by all the interested parties. For example, the designer of the refuelling system was able to see the work being done by those working on the aerodynamics of the bodywork, and vice versa. This meant that where one piece of design work might interfere with another, it was easy for those involved to see this at an early stage – consequently reducing the need for more expensive and time-consuming fixes to engineering problems that occur if the problem is discovered at a late stage. The whole team worked on a sharing basis that they considered essential (at least at the time of the visit!) to provide speed of development and reduce the time taken to eliminate problems – both of these being vital in the fast-moving world of Formula 1 car development.

Note: Organizations that encourage lateral and creative thinking, for example 3M's research function (see Chapter 5, HR) also have a better chance of recovering from problems.

And the worst?

Where there is a culture of blame and secrecy, the chances of a project disaster occurring are increased; furthermore, the chances of a disaster being reversed are decreased. This is not surprising when you think about it; an organization where management is based upon fear of losing your job is effectively hell-bent on creating disasters as well as almost guaranteeing the worst outcome in the event of one. Some argue that making an example of people in the spirit of 'pour encourager les autres' can be effective. The following is a quotation from Voltaire's *Candide*: 'Dans ce pay-ci, il est bon de tuer de temps en temps un amiral pour encourager les autres.' This translates as: 'In this country, it is good to kill an admiral from time to time, to encourage the others.' This may, or may not be helpful, but it is worth keeping in mind that in most businesses it is less often the 'admirals' and more often the workforce that pays the price – the climate of fear again.

Note: Voltaire's inspiration was the English Admiral John Byng. Sent in 1756 to prevent the French from taking Minorca, he arrived when the island was already under siege, but after an indecisive battle, disengaged after failing to relieve the siege. He was court-martialled and executed for 'failure to do his utmost'. This led to charges that he was just a scapegoat for failure higher up the chain of command. His gravestone reads 'Bravery and loyalty were insufficient securities for the life and honour of a naval officer.'

Example: Another organization had the opposite approach. It was a specialist consultancy owned by the senior managers who had set it up in conjunction with some 'sharp' investors. The permanent employees were treated badly and frequently bullied, and there was a culture of never contradicting anything said by senior staff. Where assumptions were challenged, putting the proposed project in a questionable light, retribution was rapid – contract staff were sacked and permanent staff shouted down (literally). It is perhaps unsurprising that as the project developed based on unchallenged, incorrect assumptions and so forth, things went from bad to worse. In the end, the project did fail almost completely. Once things went wrong, it was impossible to recover them in the prevailing culture.

Example: Again an example of how the wrong culture does not help. This particular organization was very top-down without much delegation. As a consequence of this culture, the design of some client documentation was changed just before it was due to be delivered. The changes concerned page layout and the adoption of a grammatically incorrect method for punctuating lists and bullet points. Although the people making this decision did not have the professional expertise to make it, as they were in charge what they said went. The consequence was a mad scramble to retrofit the documentation with the erroneous grammar. Time that should have been spent checking for errors and inconsistencies was wasted on implementing a minor change to a large volume of literature; what went out the door was not as good as it might have been.

Note: This second example also supports John Seddon's argument that command and control is the root cause of many disasters (*Freedom from Command and Control: A Better Way to Make the Work, Work*). The people making the decisions did not have the knowledge to make them, and by enforcing them via a chain of command ensured failure.

OTHER POSITIVE ORGANIZATIONAL ATTRIBUTES

As well as identifying the best culture for recovering from project disasters (or avoiding them), it is worth briefly summarizing the other positive features that have been identified.

- flexibility of response;
- financial strength;
- good financial control;
- breadth and depth of support.

Combine these with the culture, and you have a good indicator of the chances of a positive outcome from a project disaster. If the organization is lacking in more than one or two of these areas, then getting even a reasonable result will require both determination and a considerable amount of good fortune.

HOW THE PROJECT AFFECTS THE ORGANIZATION

Project disasters can impact an organization in several ways (not always negatively, but usually so). The areas of impact normally include: financial, lost opportunity, staff morale, and motivation and image. It may be any or all of these areas that are affected, depending on the scope of the disaster.

Financial

The organization sets the norms for culture and behaviour – the environment in which projects exist. However, a project disaster will impact the organization. How much will depend on the relative sizes of the project and the organization. Clearly, a US $500,000 disaster is not going to worry a billion-dollar turnover that much, though it can still make a nasty dent in the bottom line, because if the whole cost is lost it comes out of profit rather than turnover.

Example: Pre-project-disaster figures, FY 2004: turnover US $750,000 and profit US $100,000. After the project disaster, the net cost to the company was US $75,000. The revised figures are turnover US $750,000 and profit US $25,000 – a reduction in profit of 75 per cent. Of course, it is assumed here that the project would have delivered real financial benefits to the organization if it had succeeded.

Clearly the financial impact of project disasters is in the bottom line, where it has a disproportionate impact when compared to turnover, as shown in the example above. In fact, there have been cases where one major project disaster has made an otherwise sound company easy meat for a hostile takeover. Shareholders are not known for taking a long-term view. There may also be implied loss in future revenues; indeed, if a project disaster is left unresolved, i.e. abandoned to the lawyers to sort it out, then it can be a considerable time before this is forgotten.

Example: Company B, a mail-order retail organization, had a major project to deliver a web-based trading front-end. This was intended to provide additional revenue from getting focused access to the technologically aware internet community, which was expected to be a strong market for its video and hi-fi product ranges. The project failed to complete on time; in the end, it was more than six months late and cost double the original budget.

However, the costs were dwarfed by the projected loss of revenue from the missed six months of international internet trading.

Note 1: Where large organizations are split into smaller operational units, perhaps over international boundaries, the impact of a project failure can be much larger than its size might suggest. For instance, a US $50 million project within a US $1,000 million-turnover company might seem to be an issue but not the end of the world. If it were to occur within a national subsidiary with a turnover of, say, US $100 million, then the local impact may be severe.

Note 2: It is also not unheard of for cuts resulting from a major problem in the 'home' company of a multinational corporation to be visited upon the innocent 'foreign' subsidiaries. Sometimes, this even happens when the subsidiary is profitable but the parent is not – this can cause both resource and morale problems.

Lost opportunity

One of the less obvious negatives relates to the waste of resources (at least in a disaster that is not, or only partly, recovered from). Staff and material that are committed to a project cannot be used elsewhere. These resources might have been used in a directly revenue-generating role. Similarly, other projects that might have contributed to the well-being of the organization will have been delayed, or simply never started. This is particularly true where a project is for the development of a new product; here, there will very likely be wasted marketing and promotion effort too. Furthermore, in such a case, there would also be a significant penalty in terms of 'time to market'. It will usually be difficult to quantify such lost opportunity costs, and indeed it may not be helpful to do so anyway, but they can be significant.

Example: Company C had about 15 per cent of its workforce employed on a development project for a system designed to take advantage of what was considered to be a growing niche market. Unfortunately, this market was somewhat curtailed by the oil crisis in the 1970s. This meant that nearly all the research and development effort for a couple of years had been spent on something for which there was no longer a profitable market. This sort of thing is hard to foresee, and this is not a book about predicting market futures, but the consequence was that Company C found itself without anything new to build its future on; the lost opportunity cost was significant, and the company struggled to survive for several years afterwards.

Staff morale and motivation

Project failure can affect the morale of both those directly involved and others whose self-belief in the organization can be reduced. The extent of this will depend on how things are handled after the event, and will also depend on the culture of the organization concerned. Here, good line-management and HR can make all the difference; it is important that team members are re-motivated as soon as possible. In particular, it is helpful if they can be usefully employed quickly so they do not sit around dwelling on failure. (See also the section on motivation in Chapter 9.)

Note: Although a blame culture should be avoided, this does not mean that gross negligence or professional misconduct should be ignored. Indeed, where someone has, provably, caused a disaster, it is important that this is identified and that others are made aware that they were not at fault. This should be done irrespective of the fate of the guilty party.

Example: Project X failed almost completely; it was of medium profile and was intended to develop a new product. Unfortunately, the technology chosen proved to be the wrong (this was analogous to the Betamax vs VHS video standards). Those working on the project were left with no saleable end result. The organization suffered significant losses in that operating division as a consequence. However, it was appreciated that the majority of those who worked on the project had in fact worked hard and effectively. Consequently, they were not blamed for the end result, but were assessed on their actual performance; it did not count against them, and they were redeployed without impact on their career prospects. The morale in the division was preserved.

Image

The external image that an organization has, the strength of its brand, is often weakened by bad publicity from a project disaster. How this can be managed, and hopefully improved, is discussed in Chapter 6 (PR). The way in which an organization handles a project disaster can actually show it up in a good light, though this requires effort and honesty to achieve. Of course, if a disaster is turned round into a success, then this is an opportunity to improve the image; however this will not often be the case.

Case study: Coca Cola

Coca Cola embarked on an expensive project to build a plant to manufacture its 'Dasani' bottled-water brand for sale in the UK. In the United States, Dasani was the second-biggest-selling bottled water, and they expected it to do as well in the UK and Europe, where there is a strong market for bottled water. Dasani bottled water was launched in February 2004 in the UK; however, by mid-March, it had been withdrawn from the shops. The project had cost several million pounds.

The selling point for Dasani was supposed to be its purity. Unlike spa waters such as Perrier, Evian, Spa and so on, Dasani was in fact re-processed tap water, a fact that newspaper coverage made much of. Coca Cola used a process developed by NASA for purifying fluids on space vehicles. In this process, the tap water is passed through three filters that remove various impurities, such as chlorine and fine debris, followed by a technique known as reverse osmosis. This delivers water that is extremely pure. In fact, it is so pure that it is tasteless, so it is then necessary to add various impurities such as calcium, magnesium and salts to make it taste good. Because the water was sold as being so pure, it ended up being the subject of an investigation by the UK Foods Standards Agency (FSA). An article in the UK *Telegraph* (filed 19/03/2004), from which the following is an extract, appeared as a result.

A spokeswoman for the FSA said: 'Coca-Cola, the makers of Dasani, informed the Food Standards Agency yesterday that some samples of their bottled water product, Dasani, have been found to contain bromate at higher levels than are legally permitted in the UK for either bottled or tap water. Coca-Cola has advised the Agency that they are immediately withdrawing the product from sale. This is a sensible measure by the company as bromate is a chemical that could cause an increased cancer risk as a result of long-term exposure, although there is no immediate risk to public health. However, the Agency understands that some consumers may choose not to drink any Dasani they purchased prior to its withdrawal, given the levels of bromate it contains.

By March 2004, it was clear that nobody was going to buy this water, and the brand was withdrawn from the UK. Coca Cola's image was certainly damaged by the failure of the Dasani project. The common theme in this book, that most project disasters have several causes, holds true. It is hard to decide whether it was the technical fault that allowed the bromate to get into the product, the bad publicity about the source of the water, or the bad publicity about the brand that was most important in the damage that was done to Coca Cola. Image may seem to be an abstract concept, but the costs associated with having a bad image can easily exceed the direct costs of a failed project.

SUMMARY

The project and the organization in which it exists have a symbiotic relationship. What is bad for one is generally bad for the other. From the point of view of the project manager experiencing a disaster, there is little that can be done in the short term to change the culture of the organization in which the project exists. All the project manager can do is to observe and understand this culture and to make decisions that are more likely to receive support and achieve the best outcome. The organization is not so constrained; being the host for the project means that it is in a position to make or break the project by giving or withholding support. The project manager can only influence the organization's decision makers. To do this, the project manager needs to be alert to both culture and politics and to be aware of the strengths and weaknesses of the organization. This knowledge will provide the basis for promoting the right strategy; it will also provide a realistic expectation as to what can actually be achieved.

Note: It is sad, but true, that the organizational culture that is suited to getting the best outcome from a failing project is the one that is least likely to produce one in the first place. Perhaps there is some poetic justice in this, but it is surprising that such cultures are the exception, not the norm. One of the strongest blame cultures encountered by the author was in an organization with some very high-profile delivery disasters – this was not a coincidence.

CHECKLIST

Answer the questions for your project listed in Figure 7.2 and take corrective action as needed. If you are dealing with a disaster, and don't understand the corrective action that will be required, get help from someone who does. You may not have time to learn the relevant skills yourself, but at least you now know the area of ignorance; this is step one to resolving the problem.

Note: Given that the organization is larger than the project, it is unlikely that the project manager can make any significant changes to its culture, but that doesn't mean this shouldn't be tried!

Question/comment	Yes/no?
Have the strengths/weaknesses of the organization's culture been identified? – hierarchical vs delegated? – blame culture vs open? – flexible vs constrained? – any 'can-do' traits?	
Has a survival strategy been chosen that plays to the strengths? Does it: – take advantage of in-house skills? – play to organizational strengths, such as flexibility and financial resources? – directly involve the organization's actual decision-makers – obtain the support of key influencers? – take into account internal political issues? – capitalize on any commitments to deliver?	
Have mitigation plans been considered to reduce the impact of the weaknesses? – negative political situations? – non-availability of critical resources? – inflexibility? – lack of resources? – any tendency to blame?	
Has the impact of the project on the organization been analysed? – resource requirement? – financial demands/contributions? – negative image (or positive if the situation is seen to be recovered)? – personnel morale?	

Figure 7.2 Checklist: The project and the organization

8

Triumph over adversity

Up to now, this book has focused more on the causes of disasters and how they affect other parts of the organization than on what to do about them. This chapter, and the ones that follow, seeks to redress that imbalance and offers practical advice and techniques that can help. This chapter includes:

- A diagnostic approach, based upon the positive experiences of a number of people, but in particular advice from Professor John McDermid, is offered as a starting point for developing a 'get-well' strategy.
- How to make the best of the opportunities that may arise from a project disaster is discussed.
- An introduction to some useful techniques is presented.
- Some notes are included on leadership and planning.

Note: It is the case that, no matter how well you understand what is happening, what caused the disaster and the actions needed to get the best outcome, skills will be required to actually get things done. There are many books available that deal with management, leadership negotiation and other personal skills that are needed, and some of them are listed in the Bibliography. There is simply not room to provide an in-depth training manual here, nor will those experiencing a disaster first-hand have time to do too much reading.

Key point: If you identify that you don't have the right skills, get someone on board who does, fast!

The following case study is offered to underline that taking action *in extremis* can produce a positive outcome.

NASA *APOLLO 13*

No apology is made for using this case-study again; this as an example of the leadership and determination of the teams involved. The reader should not be tempted to dismiss this as being irrelevant because it was a real 'life and death' disaster; the approach taken and the skills used are transferable to the more mundane world of business projects. Previously, *Apollo 13* was used as an example of a disaster that was caused by a combination of high technology and complexity. Putting people up into space is a high-risk activity, even today. Here, the focus is on the approach that was taken to solve the problems and what skills were used to produce a good outcome.

Case study: Outbound from Earth to the Moon, an explosion in the number two oxygen tank (caused by a short circuit when the tank was 'stirred') caused severe damage to the service module, critical to getting the crew to and from the Moon. This also caused oxygen tank number one to fail. And to add to the problem, there were also problems with the fuel cells in the service module that supplied them with electrical power. The situation was serious: the command module (where the crew would normally spend most of the mission) had lost supplies of power, light and water. After about an hour and a half, it became clear that the best bet was to use the lunar landing module as a lifeboat. This was an issue in itself as the lunar module was designed to work for

45 hours, and to go round the Moon and return to Earth it would have to support the crew for 90 hours. They had plenty of oxygen; it was also calculated that they would have just enough power, but they had barely enough water – and indeed the crew set a record for the least water consumed per person per hour on a space flight. As a consequence, they were so dehydrated that the three of them lost a total of 31.5 pounds in weight – almost 50 per cent more than any other Apollo crew.

The main problem became that of carbon dioxide build-up. This led to the brain-storming/creativity session made famous in the *Apollo 13* film (*Apollo 13 'Houston, we have got a problem'*, Revelation Films Ltd, and *Apollo 13* (documentary) Classic Pictures Entertainment Ltd). Carbon dioxide is removed from the spacecraft atmosphere using lithium hydroxide canisters. The command and lunar modules carried enough of these between them; however, the square canisters from the command module were not plug-compatible with the round openings in the lunar module control system. Mission Control gave a collection of the materials that were available to the astronauts to the brainstorming team; they were allowed to use only these items to come up with a solution and then had to explain it to the crew so they could replicate it. The materials included plastic bags, tape, cardboard and the canisters themselves – they were able to solve the problem of the square peg in the round hole. A creative brainstorming solved the problem.

DIAGNOSTIC

It will not always be possible to remedy a project that is on the road to becoming a disaster. However, it is clear that many disasters have been rescued, and there are common themes to be found in the techniques applied by the rescuers. Professor John McDermid of York University is an expert in the field of information technology (IT) projects and their problems. It is fair to say that IT projects suffer from more disasters than most, so this is a rich field of study. Professor McDermid has seen many problem projects and, in an interview with the author, identified five main steps that are important in turning around a failing project. These steps are to:

1. Be honest and open about the disaster.
2. Identify the root cause(s).
3. Develop a solution;
4. Apply remedial action.
5. Implement ongoing management controls.

Although his field is IT projects, the steps are generally applicable to any complex project environment and are expanded upon here. The professor's approach is consistent with other rescue strategies discovered whilst researching this book, and suitable examples have been added to illustrate the steps and underline the themes. Quotations from the interview with Professor McDermid are marked thus: (JM).

Honesty and openness

'Don't shoot the messenger' JM
The first step is to recognize that there is a problem and to be honest and open about it. This is not always easy to do; the blame culture that is distressingly prevalent in society and in many organizations stamps down hard on those who acknowledge a problem exists. One of the reasons that GEC was successful in the United States in the 1980s was because its CEO, Jack Walsh, had a clear policy of not considering failure to be a cause for termination or other career-limiting actions. He promoted a culture that rewarded honesty and courage.

The value of this approach is underlined by contrast with a case study from a company with a totally different, blame-oriented, culture. In this example, it was clear (with 57 days to go before the project was due to be completed) that it was going to fail. However, at a critical meeting when the question was asked 'are we going to make it?', people who knew the situation looked at their immediate superiors, and when they said nothing, they chose not to say anything too – they thought it would have been career-limiting. This project ended up as an embarrassing, high-profile, public failure. It is as if a team of people who are in a boat that is in sight of the waterfall that will take them to their graves say nothing because the captain does not seem to be worried. Worse still, when the captain asks them if they think things are going well and that they will make it to the bank, they choose to say nothing because it might look bad on their record to cast doubt on the soundness of the leadership.

Indeed, it is the difficulty of admitting that something is wrong that is one of the causes of project disasters in the first place. If a problem is caught early enough, then its cure tends to be less expensive and simpler than if it is left until much later.

Example: Considering the case study on the de Havilland Comet, it is worth noting contemporary quotes from the *Herald Tribune* and *Time* magazine. From the former: 'full marks to Britain for its brutally honest and frank enquiry'; from the latter: 'British science has told the world without excuse or cover up what happened to their proudest airliner, the ill-starred jet Comet.' These quotes were produced in response to the published findings of the RAE (Royal Aircraft Establishment) enquiry, headed by Sir Arnold Hall, into the causes of the explosive decompression crashes of two Comet 1s in 1954. This enquiry highlighted the limited understanding of metallurgy that led to metal-fatigue failures. The whole world was able to learn from this investigation, and it is likely that many lives have been saved as a result. The openness and honesty that de Havilland and the RAE showed gained them both substantial enhanced reputations in the industry and in the public eye.

Example: *Apollo 13* again, the famous radio call, 'Houston, we've had a problem', meets the honesty and open criterion. The crew immediately informed Mission Control that something had happened and went about making sure that everything they knew was passed on. This was the first step in what turned out to be one of the most famous recoveries from a disaster on record.

Identification of root causes

'Review – not audit' JM.
When reviewing the state of a project that is in difficulties, it is important not to approach it as if you were an auditor seeking to find fault; the 'blame' problem again. To do so will only generate hostility and this will not help move matters forward. This is particularly true where someone from the outside is brought in to help with the problem. They are not part of the team; they can be seen as a threat, and if they take an audit-like approach, then people will quite likely hide information to protect themselves.

What is needed is a review, preferably one that gives the equivalent of an external view of the project. The goal is to identify what has been done, what has not been done, what was planned for/not and so on.

'Don't look for a single cause – keep looking' JM.
This assessment that the cause of a disaster is not always simple is borne out by the experience of air-accident investigation specialists (such as the United State's NTSB and the UK's AAIB). Their work shows that there is often a complex set of interactive factors involved in an air crash. The reason for this is that aviation is a complex business; similarly, as discussed in Chapter 1, a key feature of projects is that they are complex. So, it is not surprising that when investigating a project disaster you need to take the same forensic approach as an air-accident investigator and not be surprised if the cause is not obvious. Indeed, it is important to keep investigating until you are sure every contributory factor has been identified. The same applies to project disasters; when analysing what went wrong, don't leap on the first possible cause that comes along – it is unlikely to be the only problem.

Development of a solution

In turning around a failing project, there are four key variables: scope, time, resources and quality. Anyone trying to attempt a rescue will need to consider all of these and may well end up having to work on all of them to obtain a good result. There is often a degree of interaction between them; for example, having insufficient resources may show itself as a lack of time.

Note: Heisenburg's Uncertainty Principle was originally postulated for quantum-scaled particles; you can know where they are, or how fast they are moving, but not both. This can also apply to some projects; you can know what the exact scope is, but be uncertain as to how much time it would take to deliver. The same goes for any combination of the four parameters described above.

Scope

What can we throw away?' JM.

This is the first question that should be asked when reviewing the scope of a project in the throes of disaster. It can be further refined as below.

- What elements are essential core components without which nothing else can be delivered?
- Which elements can be delivered most quickly?

The mantra should be 'greatest business benefits first'. The scope should not be trimmed somewhere just because it is easy to do so at that point; the priority needs to be related to customer needs.

Time

'Artificial vs real deadlines' JM.

It is very easy to get carried away with meeting internal deadlines. The author worked on a large project in the education sector where some of the senior management were very focused on meeting internal deadlines generated by the project plan and would interfere, and more importantly 'micro-manage' if they heard that this was happening. Their interference invariably had a negative impact on both staff morale and resource utilization. Disproportionate effort was spent on trying to meet the internal deadline to the detriment of the client deliverables. It is important to identify which are real deadlines, on the critical path to client delivery, and which are simply internal milestones that may be useful for measuring progress but are not critical in themselves.

Resources

There are two main issues here; having enough resources and having the right resources. Both of these are important; having too much of the wrong resource is almost as useless as having no resources at all ('almost' because you may be able to trade your wrong resource with someone else's right resource). It is always tempting to throw additional resources at a project. Sadly, this does not work. The traditional analogy is people digging a hole – there is only so much room for them to dig in.

Case study: First World War

There is an apocryphal story, commonly believed but disputed by many historians, that General Haig's staff's analysis was that as the male population of fighting age available to the Allies was greater than that of the enemy, then a war of attrition was the way to go. As long there were allied soldiers left alive after the entire enemy forces had perished, then we would win. History shows that this led only to wholesale slaughter, and in the end it was technology and better tactics that brought the war to a close. Simply throwing more resources at the problem meant that for years, the battlefront moved a matter of yards despite the great loss of life. The more trivial, and less controversial, example of how many people you can get into a hole to speed-up digging it is perhaps better. No matter how many labourers you have, you can only get so many of them into the hole at one time; what's more, they get in each other's way and slow things up!

Having the correct resources is also critical to recovering a project. 'Correct' needs to be determined in terms of quantity, skill set and ability.

Quality

'Good enough, not perfection' JM

In some projects, the problem is too much 'quality' – the project is drowning in quality reviews and documents. However, in more cases, the problem is insufficient quality – there is insufficient checking to ensure that what is delivered is what was required. As defined in PRINCE 2, the quality plan for the project (if there isn't one as with risk plans, the question should be asked 'Why not?' – this is a significant omission) is there to ensure that the deliverables are:

- fit for the purpose;
- conformant to their requirements;
- designed and produced to do the job properly;
- able to meet the customer requirements.

As with documentation, it can often be tempting to abandon quality-related activities when things are rough. A better solution is to review what quality is needed as a minimum to support the robust delivery of the project, even if that means adding work rather than removing it. As a minimum, this will usually include quality responsibilities, product descriptions, standards to be used, methods to be used, and some form of test plan.

Remedial action

By now, the shortcomings of the project should have been identified; why things are in trouble should be known. If not, then it is time to revisit the points raised so far – or get help from someone who can perhaps do the job more objectively. Assuming that the cause (causes, more likely) is known, it is time to take remedial action to get the best possible outcome. What this boils down to is having a plan that says who is going to do what, when and how and communicating the new deliverables and timetable to the client. This will often be an iterative process; negotiation is going to play a significant part here. It will be vital to be able show that any remedial action proposed would have a high probability of success. Credibility is all at this point; there is very little chance of being given another opportunity if the remedial action fails. For PR reasons, it may be necessary to have the remedial action plan presented, and possibly managed, by someone other than the original project manager. Not only must it work, but also the client must be happy with its method of delivery. It is worth keeping in mind that most clients will be more interested in realizing the benefits of a project than the methods used to deliver them.

Example: Lateral thinking

A European world wide web- (internet-) based commerce system was due to go live by an imminent date. The client part of the system, where the customers chose what they wished to buy was complete, and the 'back-office' component that arranged for goods to be dispatched, invoices sent, payments processed and so forth existed. Unfortunately, the glue that was to link the two systems together was not going to be completed until some time after the announced 'go live' date. As nothing was possible without this 'glue', the project certainly met the criteria for being a disaster. An external consultant was called in and came up with the interim solution of having temporary administrators print off orders from the client system and then re-type them into the 'back-office' system. As transaction volumes were expected to be fairly low for the first few weeks of trading, this bought the necessary time to allow the 'glue' to be completed. There were costs associated with this, but the end result was that the system appeared to be complete as far as the outside world was concerned and enabled the project to meet its deadlines.

Ongoing management and methods

Assuming that a disaster has been partially or wholly recovered, now is the time to put measures in place to stop it happening again. It is not enough to fix the problems that have occurred; it is important to cure their causes, particularly if they were down to poor management. Ideally, these should be industry standard and proven; it helps if tools are used that can be understood by a wide audience. This makes resource acquisition and communication that much easier. Some methodologies are so complex that by the time anyone has learned to use them, a new disaster will have taken place.

Typically, any methods adopted need to provide for the following:

- *Reports*: simple and clear identification of trends and progress;
- *Objectives and requirements*: these must be clearly communicated and understandable;
- *Deliverables*: clearly identified internal and external deliverables;
- *Change*: a mechanism for identifying, controlling, authorizing and monitoring change;
- *Risk*: must support the identification, assessment, planning and monitoring of new/ongoing risks;
- *Tasks*: it must be possible for a single person to identify every element of work needed;
- *Measurements*: there must be measurements (simple) that can be used to establish if the project is meeting its objectives (if you can't measure it, then you can't know if it is complete).

OPPORTUNITIES

There are those who say 'there are no problems, only opportunities.' These people must be very happy whenever they get close to a disaster. Whatever the reader's views on such a philosophy, or trite catchphrase, are, there is evidence to support the existence of opportunities within disasters. In the UK, the Millennium Dome project was widely accepted to be a disaster (though at the time this was such a political, with a large 'P', project that getting an admission of that would have been hard). It suffered greatly from being set up and run by a committee of the great and the good, who had no real expertise in running what was more like a fairground attraction than anything else. In fact, things were so bad that new management was acquired in the form of the ex Euro Disney manager Pierre Yves Gerbeau. For him, it was a great opportunity and took him from relative obscurity to at least Europe-wide recognition. He was able to make the project reach completion in time for the Millennium (a very real deadline). Opinions vary as to whether or not the end result was great or awful, but the disaster was averted and the project completed. Note that this was not a civil engineering problem; the structure worked well, but there was an issue with its use and the delivery of the 'Millennium Experience' project – which ended up over-budget (and seen by considerably fewer visitors than had been forecast).

The key opportunities for people and organizations that stem from a disaster come from one of three things. Turning the project around (phoenix from the ashes), making the decision to stop it (preventing the throwing of good money after bad) and seeing a completely new possibility (the lateral approach). In this chapter, an example of each of these is presented; no guarantee is offered that readers will be able to do the same themselves, but these are the outcomes that provide the best opportunities. Perhaps this chapter should be subtitled with a quote from Monty Python's *Life of Brian* 'always look on the bright side of life.'

Note: The examples given here also fit into the same categories outlined in earlier chapters. What is important in these instances is the recognition of opportunities amongst the wreckage.

Phoenix from the ashes

Looking for different uses for a project/product can reap rewards. This example is taken from a project to produce a product for retail manufacturing that took place in the late 1970s. It was not so much that the original project failed, but that the reasons for its existence disappeared.

Note: The author is not aware if such legislation still applies anywhere in Europe (or the United States for that matter).

Case study: The project was based upon meeting consumer legislation that would require a different method of defining what was in a packet sold to the public. At the time, the standard method was to say that if a packet stated that it contained a fixed weight or volume, for example 100 grams, then it must contain at least that. Anything less, and the supplier could be prosecuted or fined. A new approach, already in use in another country, specified a statistical measure whereby a batch of products should have none less than a certain percentage below the stated weight/volume; the average weight should be at or above that stated. In fact, it was slightly more complex than this, but that does not matter here. This was not good news for retail manufacturers who were faced with a change from simply weighing each package and rejecting any that were light to one where they had to record the weight of each package, keep records, and apply the appropriate analysis to prove compliance. The organization concerned realized that this was an opportunity for a new product to use computer technology to record the information and provide the reports and evidence required automatically. It also saw that it could use the technology to control the packing equipment to ensure that the packets were filled to an appropriate level to meet the requirements for minimum weight. Consequently, a project was set up to produce such a system that would enable the retail manufacturer to meet the forthcoming regulation at the same time as minimizing the 'over-pack' needed to ensure that the lower limit was not breached. The project went well and a prototype system was produced. It worked well and would have met the proposed regulations.

However, successful lobbying by manufacturers and pressure groups who felt that the public would not accept a system where they might 'get less than they thought they were paying for' meant that the new regulation was abandoned. This certainly comes under the category of a major project disaster – there was now no reason for the project to exist or continue. It looked as though all the resources spent were wasted – this was a blow. At this point somebody, in marketing it is alleged, realized that a feature of the system was that as well as ensuring that the regulations were met it also ensured that the minimum 'over-pack' would be achieved. It was realized that this could still be applied to a production line where the goal was exceeding a minimum target weight (for example 100 grams). The manufacturer benefited from putting in as little extra product as possible over the target. This represented a real saving for a volume manufacturer and provided a degree of success for what might have been a written-off project.

This case study illustrates a good point: the original goals for a project may change, but what has been achieved may still be of real use. It is admitted that this is more likely to be the case where a project exists to produce what is effectively a product than it is for a totally bespoke solution. However, it may well be the case that components created to support a bespoke solution may well have applications elsewhere. Smart organizations will look to do this for components from successful projects as well as from failed ones; the more return that can be obtained from a development investment, the better.

Other examples of the 'phoenix from the ashes' include:

- the de Havilland Comet airliner, which after initial problems (see Chapter 2 for more details on this) went on to be a successful venture;
- the Millennium Bridge over the Thames, which required engineering shortcomings (it made people feel sea sick) to be rectified before its benefits could be realized.

Don't throw good money after bad

Assuming that the budget has not all been spent, or over-spent as may well be the case, then looking for a new place to invest the remainder is a good idea. In practice, most terminated projects have what budget is left clawed back into the organization; the same goes for the human and equipment resources.

Example: Project Y for a television facilities organization, in the 1980s, had reached the point of no return; the product to which it related showed little potential for further sales using the existing technology. It was either a case of start the development from scratch or cancel. That it was in trouble had been recognized and the process of bringing matters to a halt was well advanced. Arguably, this was not a real disaster, just a case of a product nearing the end of its life cycle. However, for those involved it was bad news. Meanwhile, local management had identified that some of the money and some of the resources could usefully be applied to a new project. The original project related to the development of 'frame store' technology as part of a video-effects system that was being overtaken by competing technologies. It was decided to further develop the hardware technology of the frame store instead of developing the whole product. It was established that there was a third-party market for such devices, and so good money was channelled in that direction. The organization not only stopped the waste of money but also could arguably be included in the 'phoenix from the ashes' category as well.

Note: a frame store is a device that is capable of holding a captured still-video image in computer memory. Once there, the image can be edited and effects added before it is either moved into long-term storage, such as a computer disk, or converted back into analogue video signals for display.

Lateral approach

Here, the trick is to look for an alternative approach that allows the project to deliver what is required using other means/resources than was originally intended. The author made himself unpopular with an employer at one time by taking a lateral-thinking approach to a client's problem. This led to loss of business in the short term, looked on as a bad thing! However, in the longer term, it built credibility with the client.

Example: This took place in the early 1980s; technology was more expensive and bandwidth less available than it is today, and indeed the story would not be credible today. A railway had a central and a regional computer data centre. To keep these in step with each other, and to provide a back-up of data, a magnetic tape was sent by train twice a day from the regional to the central location. Sadly, about one in four of these tapes failed to make the journey for a variety of reasons; this was a major nuisance for the railway company. The author, in a sales role, met with one of the railway data centres with a view to fulfilling a need to put in a data link between the two centres. The idea was to have a mini-computer at each data centre that communicated with the other via a leased-line data communications link. There would have been a cost of more than £10,000 for the computers (plus installation, maintenance and so forth) and a significant annual cost for the data link. The alternative suggestion proposed was simply to make two tapes and send the duplicate via a motor-cycle courier (or on different train). This was significantly cheaper and was seized upon with alacrity by the client. Not a good result from a sales viewpoint, but good for the business relationship.

The following case study shows where a lateral-thinking approach enabled a project disaster to be averted.

Case study: This example has already been referred to in Chapter 7. However, it is given here, with a different slant, to illustrate where creative thinking saved the day. This was an IT project that was being put together about the time of the 'dot-com' boom in the 1990s. A mail-order company with a significant catalogue sales organization planned to make this available to the world via the internet. It already had a 'back-office' IT solution that allowed it to process payments and organize deliveries and so forth. It also had a stock-control and checking system and a telesales organization. What it didn't have was an internet, web-based sales front-end or the 'glue' to connect this to the existing systems. This was needed so that an internet customer could choose an item from the catalogue, check that it was available, pay for it and arrange delivery. A programme consisting of the projects needed to deliver the missing components was set in place.

Unfortunately, although the 'front-end' system was completed in good time to meet the date – the service had been advertised as being available to the outside world – the 'glue' was not. The reasons for the failure of the 'glue' project are not important here; it is sufficient to know that it could not have been rescued in an acceptable time. What mattered was that the service had been widely promoted to the outside world. Its non-appearance would have two main consequences: the company/brand would be damaged and a time-to-market advantage would be lost to competitors. After some brain-storming, a lateral approach was adopted using the materials to hand (see also the *Apollo 13* solution). The solution was to use the manual input system for the telesales function to take the information coming out of the internet sales system. Administrative personnel were able to print out the orders/enquires and key them into the existing 'back-end system'. These staff could also key responses into the internet front-end and send them to the customers. This was not a cheap solution, but it was possible to put it in place quickly, buying time for the 'glue' to be completed. The organization did not lose face, or time to market. It did lose money, but only in the short term. The project manager gained a good reputation for saving the day.

Being creative and looking for an alternative approach, or an opportunity, can work and has worked in the past. It is reasonable to expect that it will do so again in the future.

Note: An excellent example of lateral thinking can also be found in the humble Post-it™ Note. In 1968, the inventor, Dr Spencer Silver, a senior scientist in 3M's Corporate Research Lab, discovered a unique adhesive that could be re-positioned. This was not necessarily the original intention, but he set out to see if any of his colleagues had a use for it. Nothing happened until, in 1974,

Art Fry, another 3M scientist, wanted a movable, but sticky, bookmark for the music he sang in a choir. He recalled Silver's glue and the rest is history; after widespread use within 3M, they reached the outside world in the late 1970s. It is almost impossible to imagine a world without such notes; the author used them extensively when editing this book.

Learn from it

Perhaps the most obvious opportunity that any project disaster offers those involved, and their organization and customers, is to learn form it. It may seem trivial to mention this, but people associated with a disaster often wish simply to forget all about it. This is a terrible waste of experience; the lessons available could easily help prevent the next project disaster. That UK Government IT projects keep failing in similar ways suggests that this is something that may not be being done!

Any organization that gets to the end of a disaster should, as a matter of course, hold a thorough debriefing to identify the following:

- the causes;
- what was done well;
- what was done badly;
- what could have been done (that wasn't) to avert the disaster;
- what was done (that shouldn't have been) that made things get worse;
- what could have been done to improve the outcome;
- how can it be prevented next time.

It is important to try and keep the blame culture at bay for this exercise if the real lessons to be learnt are to be identified. A witch-hunt will result in defensive behaviour that will not help the truth to be discovered.

On the negative side

Not all lessons to be learned relate to positive outcomes; for example, poor documentation and training are frequent causes of severe problems in the future.

Documentation

It is also worth noting that when a project is under pressure (time or money), it is often the documentation that is the first casualty. Even if the troubled project survives, this can be the sown seed for the next disaster down the line. A future project may set off to produce something new based on the earlier work, only to discover that vital information simply does not exist – the people involved have left the organization. To all intents and purposes, the original project may just as well have been completed using a magic wand.

Training

Again, when times are hard, it is also tempting to cut down on the training for those who are to use the end result. This is especially true for IT projects where good implementations have failed because the human element has been ignored. The Child Support Agency has been cited as an example of this – the new system (date) was not simply a replacement for the previous one, but with better performance it required a different approach to working altogether. This was not taken fully into account, and has been given as a significant factor in the failures of this agency.

Summary of opportunities

It may be over optimistic to assume that if you make the right decisions, a disaster can be turned into success. However, as the examples show, things can turn out for the better. Part of the secret is to de-focus from the immediate problem, however hard that may be, and take a wider view. It is a good disaster-survival strategy to be on the look out for an opportunity to achieve something positive, even if the project itself is doomed.

USEFUL TECHNIQUES

As mentioned in the introduction to this chapter, it quickly became clear that there were specific skills needed to help a failing project into recovery.

Brain-storming

The value of taking time out to review what is actually happening in a project that is in a mess is a common theme when researching this book and seems well established. As shown in Figure 8.1, one of the best ways to do this is to run a brain-storming meeting, as the freedom and flexibility of such meetings gives a good chance of hitting on a novel solution (or an obvious one that people have been just too stressed to spot).

There are many variants on how a brain-storming session should be done, and several excellent and not-so-excellent books telling you how to run them. There are also training courses, though it is probable that if you have time to go on one, then there isn't a disaster in progress. However, because it is such a useful technique, a brief overview/recipe is provided here for the benefit of the uninitiated.

SWOT

As with brain-storming, another useful analytical tool is SWOT. This stands for strengths, weaknesses, opportunity and threats. It is more often found in the sales and marketing arena, but it can help identify the way forward for a project team too. The process

Step	Description
1 Initiation	Call the meeting – determine who can usefully contribute; it is suggested that you have no fewer than 3 people and no more than 12 or things will get out of hand. If possible, get people outside of the immediate project team to provide an outside view. Only ask people who have relevant experience and skills; avoid senior managers who wish to be there solely because they are 'important'.
2 Location	Choose a venue, preferably away from the normal place of work, that can comfortably take the size of meeting and has a ready supply of tea/coffee plus white board and plenty of flip charts with associated pens and the like. If you like, consider video-recording the whole process to make sure nothing gets lost.
3 Set-up	Make sure all those attending know what the meeting is for, where and when it is and what the topic is. Provide briefing notes on brain-storming if necessary. Set up the room and make sure any equipment works, there are flip-chart pens that work, Blu Tack for sticking charts to the wall and so forth. Check there are enough chairs, and once everyone arrives, get them settled down with mobile phones turned off.
4 Meeting	The meeting will typically have four stages: (a) Briefing – who is doing what, restriction on scope, areas of interest. (b) 'Brain-storming' – record thoughts and suggestions without any attempt at analysis/comment – anything from 15 minutes to an hour or so. Don't worry if people say the same thing twice, or similar things, just get everything written down without comment. Use of flip charts is a good idea (white boards are difficult to take away afterwards), ideally with someone who can write neatly to capture the ideas. (c) Analysis/discussion. There are different ways of doing this; one is to group the ideas to give structure and remove duplicates and then quickly prioritize those that look most promising for discussion. The ideas are then discussed to

Figure 8.1 Brain-storming

Step	Description
	determine if they are helpful, what should be done next, etc. It is important not to try and work out how you would implement any ideas in detail, as either the meeting will never end or the first ideas get debated well, but the later ones not at all. The discussions need to be recorded. (d) What next – agree on who will do what to progress the remaining useful ideas. It may be that some ideas need further brain-storming. It is worth keeping the original flip charts and ideas for the time being as sometimes what was rejected initially may come in useful later on.
5 Follow-up	Hopefully, the meeting will have come up with some original, and maybe even project-saving, ideas. These will inevitably require some effort to put them into progress, and it is important to make sure that what happens next is documented and followed up.

Figure 8.1 Brain-storming (*continued*)

is straightforward: for each of the categories, you identify what these are for the project in question. A good way to do this is to adopt a brain-storming approach for each one in turn. In the sales arena, this would then be done for the competitors to help identify where a competitive advantage could be gained; in a project, it might be helpful to do this for the project's needs and for the project team to find gaps (it is possible to complement this with a brain-storming session on the project's needs). Once the brain-storming session has been completed, it is then useful to score each section, perhaps between one and five, to give it a quantitative measure. For instance, the project team may have in-depth technical knowledge of stress analysis for concrete structures and might merit a 5; the project may use very little stressed-concrete structures, and this could be regarded as a weakness (1). A simplified SWOT chart is shown in Figure 8.2.

Strengths do not always map onto weaknesses, but it can be helpful to group them during the analysis. Such a table can be

Strength	Weakness
Because project is high profile, a budget is available to obtain additional support externally.	No testing and quality-assurance skills available to the team in the organization.
Opportunity	**Threat**
HR department's expertise in obtaining contract staff provides chance to obtain staff without diverting project team from current activities.	Time available to develop credible recovery plan (specified by client) is only 5 days.

Figure 8.2 Simplified SWOT chart

helpful in finding out what to do next, or at the very least help define where help is needed first.

Note: For a complex project, it may be helpful to 'SWOT' separate parts of the project in separate sessions, e.g. technical, commercial, subcontractors and so on.

Plans

There are many planning tools (such as PERT and Gantt charts, flow charts, software packages) available to help manage a project; some are listed in the glossary included in the Introduction). Plans typically take some form of work-breakdown structure (WBS) associated with a means of specifying sequence and timescale (this is where Gantt and PERT become helpful). The suggestions below are aimed at producing the best workable plan in the shortest time.

Planning

It is usually easiest to plan from the 'top down'. Start with high-level chunks of work, for example 'produce technical solution', then break them down into components and subcomponents as required, until a task that has only one person responsible for delivering it is reached. This produces a WBS that should cover the whole project. However, this does not cover sequence/dependency – it is also necessary for every item to establish what must be done before it starts (and, it follows, to specify what can't be done until it is finished). This will often require a combination of top-down and bottom-up methods.

Estimating

Closely associated with planning is estimating. If you don't know how long an activity will take or what resource are needed to deliver it, then it is difficult to have a realistic plan. It is often easiest to form estimates on a 'bottom-up' approach, ie to make estimates for what are single, discrete tasks that are the responsibility of a single person. These can then be fed into the WBS/network of the plan to come up with a timetable and a budget.

Iteration

Apart from the fact that the first plan/estimate often comes up with an unacceptable combination of timescale and budget for a given specification (see Nickson's *Corollary*), it will normally be the case that the plan goes through a number of iterations. Of course, it will need to be revisited with change and completion of the project over time. This is important if it is to represent reality; however, there is a pragmatic judgement to be made between the detail of the plan vs time and the amount of effort needed to keep it up to date.

Note: Effective planning requires both a bottom-up and a top-down approach if a workable end result is to be obtained – using just the one method does not produce reliable plans.

Leadership

First of all, what is it? Donnald H McGannon defined it as follows: 'Leadership is action, not position.' In other words, the job title is not what makes you a team leader; it is what you say and do and the example you set. Concrete advice on leadership comes from General George S Patton 'Never tell people how to do things, tell them what to do and they will surprise you with their ingenuity.' This is something that the author has seen time and time again where the most technically able are put in charge of a programming team. Instead of setting clear goals and objectives for their team, they spend ages looking at their code and telling them how they would have done it. This not only has the effect of wasting everyone's time, but also creates considerable animosity between the leader and the led.

One of the first skills that must be acquired to become a successful team leader is that of setting objectives. You cannot expect people to do a job for you unless they are clear as to what they are supposed to be doing; they must know what the team, and individual, objectives are.

SMART

There is a short acronym SMART (simple, measurable, achievable, realistic, time frame) that is commonly used to help in objective setting (see also note in Chapter 2 'Why project disasters happen'). In this, any objective is defined in such a way as to meet the criteria. For example, asking your nephew to wash the car by 17.00 today, might not fit the bill if asked at 16.50. The objective is simple (to obtain a clean car), it is measurable (the dirt is gone!), it is not, however, achievable in the timetable with the available resources (a bucket of water and one nephew).

Once you have checked out the objectives against the SMART test, then you must establish how you, in your role as team leader, will implement them. Rudyard Kipling's 'I keep six honest serving men (They taught me all I knew); their names are What and

Why and When, and How and Where and Who' can serve you well here. For example, the following questions are typical of those you should ask yourself; you will be able to think of more yourself along the same theme:

- What resource are needed to get the work done? What are the external dependencies?
- Why do we need to do this? Why is it important?
- When do we need to start/complete the work? When do we need to tell other teams that we have completed it?
- How do I motivate the team to do it? How do we measure it? How will it affect other objectives?
- Where do I get the resources, where will they sit?
- Who is going to help me? Who needs to know what actions I am taking? Who will benefit from the objective being achieved?

This may seem time-consuming, but like preparation time spent before cooking a meal, it makes a tremendous difference to the finished result and to the amount of dirty pans (or plans) left over at the end.

Once the team objectives are established, then it is possible to define those for the individual team members. Again, the SMART criteria apply in exactly the same way. Each individual must know what they are going to do, how it is to be measured, that it is something that can be done in the time available, and that the resources they require are accessible to them.

KISS

Related to SMART is KISS; this stands for 'keep it simple sir'. In other words, don't make things complicated when they don't need to be. If something is complex, then break it down into elements that aren't. It is rare that this isn't possible, and it is always desirable.

Key points: Project leaders:

● Team objectives clearly set?
● Is it SMART?
● Individual goals defined?
● What, why, when, how, where, and who – is this known?

If not, then try again until they are; anything else is likely to fail.

Note: See also Appendix 1, on teams, for further background material relating to team management.

SUMMARY

This chapter is intended to help find a way forward from an impending, or evolving, project disaster. The assumption is that prevention is no longer an option; the old Irish saying 'I wouldn't be starting from here' probably applies. However, stepping back and looking at the options available and considering any opportunities that may present themselves and employing any appropriate techniques described here should help achieve a better outcome.

CHECKLIST

The checklist presented in Figure 8.3 covers only the recovery methods described in this chapter; it does not cover the sections on skills. Answer the following questions for your project and take corrective action as needed. If you are dealing with a disaster, and don't understand the corrective action that will be required, get help from someone who does. You may not have time to learn the relevant skills yourself, but at least you now know the area of ignorance; this is step one to resolving the problem.

Question/comment	Yes/no?
Applying the diagnostics have you: – been honest and open about the disaster? – identified the root causes? – developed a workable solution? – applied remedial action? – implemented ongoing management controls?	
Have the options been identified for: – resources? – scope? – time? – quality?	
Is it possible to define and develop a solution based on these options?	
Were the following considered when developing the solution: – avoiding throwing good money after bad? – looking for a lateral approach? – learning from events? – brain-storming? – SWOT? – KISS (particularly for objectives)?	
Do the management methods adopted provide: – reports? – objectives and requirements? – identified deliverables? – change management? – risk management? – identified tasks to the level of one person, one job? – measurements for progress?	

Figure 8.3 Checklist for use of diagnostics

9

Recipes and survival skills

The message that this book has set out to deliver is that 'project disasters happen, but there are things that can be done to get the best possible outcome. They can sometimes be survived!' This chapter looks at various recipes and diagnostics that have been used when faced with a project disaster. There is also a checklist that can be adopted to assess the best course of action. In addition, some skills that have been useful in such situations are included in outline for use *in extremis*. This is a 'hands-on' chapter and has been written with ease of use and assimilation in mind, not rigour.

Note: Further suggestions for dealing with problems within teams are given in Appendix 1.

RECIPES

There are four main recipes considered; do nothing, start again, admit defeat, review and continue. Of course, there is also the option of getting it right in the first place, and that is considered too, but in that case this chapter would probably not be being read. The benefits of these are summarized here to help make a choice, though it is important to note that not all project disasters will support all these strategies. In some cases, it may be necessary to adopt different approaches for different parts of the project. Keep in mind that just because the project is a disaster does not mean that it is all being done wrong or in the same way. The negative implications of some of these strategies are covered in the final chapter – what not to do. Readers are also invited to look at Chapter 3, 'Learning from disasters', where there are further examples of these strategies being employed, and their outcomes.

Note: A common point made which applies to any of these strategies is to avoid getting lawyers involved as a means of resolving a disaster unless absolutely needed. As with divorce, once lawyers are actively involved on an adversarial basis, it is very unlikely that matters can be brought to an amicable and successful outcome. Getting advice as to the legal position is, on the other hand, useful.

Do nothing

This seldom if ever works, but it does seem to have been tried on a number of occasions. It usually happens because people try to pretend that the disaster is not happening in the first place, or because they are too flummoxed to think of anything. The author is not aware of any instance where this has worked; however, it must have happened somewhere. Of course, if the project's disaster is because of an external event, such as the bankruptcy of the parent organization, there may be nothing else that can be done. In such cases, it will be clear that there is nothing to do but wait until the situation is resolved (see Figure 9.1).

Start again from scratch

Starting again from scratch means effectively throwing away everything done to date – hopefully, with the exception of lessons learnt (see Figure 9.2). This can, and has worked. It tends to be

Benefit	Commentary
Requires no action	It is hard to see that there are any benefits of taking this approach. By adopting this course of inaction, you are not so much grasping at straws as hoping a straw will fall into the palm of your hand for you to hold on to. This is not a safe bet, but can be seductive because it fits in with a strategy of denial.

Figure 9.1 Doing nothing

expensive, it is wasteful, and it requires a flexible timetable. It has been seen to work within a larger programme where the project was not yet on the critical path for overall delivery. It comes with a health warning that, because time has passed, the project will be operating in a new environment – just fixing the problems that cause the disaster the first time round will not necessarily guarantee a good outcome this time.

Benefit	Commentary
Learn from failure	By starting again, the new project can at least see where the previous attempt went wrong and avoid that error. This does not mean that a new error may not occur, or, in some cases, that the old ones will not be repeated.
Revalidated goals	The opportunity to re-establish what the project is for, what it needs to achieve and what its timetable and deliverables are should not be undervalued. This is particularly valuable, as poorly defined project goals are in themselves a common cause of project disasters.
A clean sheet	Starting from scratch means that the new project is not tarred with the same brush as the original project. It can be seen as having a clean sheet. A new team can distance itself from the baggage accumulated during the failure.

Figure 9.2 Starting again from scratch

Admit defeat

Admitting defeat is not as awful as it sounds. By admitting that the situation is unrecoverable, it becomes possible to communicate this effectively so that the consequences can be established (see Figure 9.3). The parent organization can then make sensible plans and not carry on in the false belief that all is well. It gives the opportunity to establish the cause of the failure, learn what lessons can be learnt and plan for the future. If the project really is unrecoverable, then recognizing it means that new thinking can begin. The downside is that it becomes all too easy for the blame game to start here. Not all disasters are someone's fault, and even if they are it is often not the most effective strategy to blame someone, sack them or otherwise punish them. Doing so also tends to limit the ability of the organization to build upon any lessons learnt and to show to the outside world that it is doing so. There are also motivational benefits to be gained by supporting staff who may have failed but can grow as a result. This is not the same as encouraging failure.

Benefit	Commentary
Limits loss	By stopping the project, further waste is avoided, though it is inevitable that, apart from any lessons learnt, all the previous effort is simply lost. It does mean that any benefits a successful project may have delivered will not be realized.
Draws a line	Stopping the project does at least give everyone, and the organization, the chance to put a full stop after an unhappy sentence. People get the chance to lick their wounds and get on with something new.
New opportunities	Because financial, material and human resources are no longer committed to the failing project, there is the chance to use them elsewhere, hopefully to positive effect. It minimizes the lost opportunity cost.

Figure 9.3 Admitting defeat

Review and continue

Reviewing and continuing involves recognizing that events are out of immediate control and that things cannot carry on as before. This has been seen to be the best option in most cases. It has all the advantages of *admitting defeat* and *starting again*. In addition, it has the further benefits listed in Figure 9.4.

Get it right in the first place

John Seddon, one of the people canvassed by the author, is of the view that most disasters, if not all, occur because the projects are not entered into based upon the right knowledge in the first place. Projects should be based upon a clear knowledge of what is actually required, and the implementation decision should be made by people with the appropriate knowledge to do the work. Following this approach will reduce the number of project disasters (see Figure 9.5). It can also be argued that if a project is run honestly and effectively using one of the more traditional project methodologies (such as PRINCE 2), then it should be possible to achieve a much higher success rate than is currently the case. Irrespective of whether the reader accepts Seddon's approach that project disasters are a consequence of command and control thinking, it is obviously the case that having the wrong goals for a project and/or having the wrong people working on it is not a good idea!

METHOD

The following method is provided as a first step for those finding themselves in the midst of a disaster. Simply taking the time out to ask yourself these questions may well allow the wood to be distinguished from the trees. This method checklist is aimed at project managers, but it can be used by anyone to support a case

Benefit	Commentary
Less waste	Because the project team, equipment, resources and work done to date are kept (as far as possible), this approach reduces the waste implicit in the earlier strategies. However, to some extent this may be illusory as the continuing project may not keep all the 'work' that was done before, and some activities may be repeated.
Project continuity	Assuming the same team (or some of the original team) is involved in the ongoing project, then any knowledge they have gained, lessons learnt and so forth are available for the remainder of the project. This should save familiarization time when compared with a new project. Admittedly, if the reason for the problem was the wrong staff or incompetent staff, then the problems will surely recur.
Improving morale	Should be good for morale, as people do not like giving up on a problem. Staff can be re-motivated and given fresh impetus to succeed.
Positive image	The organization is seen to have turned around a problem, and this will make up for its getting in a mess in the first place. There is always credibility in seeing things through to a positive conclusion.
Customer satisfaction	By seeing things through, the client may be more sympathetic to problems than they would have been with other approaches. Solving problems builds confidence.

Figure 9.4 Reviewing and continuing

Benefit	Commentary
No disaster	It is obvious that getting the project right means there is no disaster – this book would not be necessary if this were more common.

Figure 9.5 Getting it right in the first place

for remedial action. It can also be used in conjunction with the more detailed 'recovery approach' given in Chapter 8.

Step 1: Identify the cause(s)

Which of the following apply?

- Have any external events occurred that make the project non-viable?
- Are the goals unclear, or do different people have different understandings of the goals?
- Are the goals the right ones for the project (either now or when it started)?
- Does the project depend on high-risk/unproven technology to deliver the goals?
- Is the project sufficiently and correctly resourced?
- Has there been a failure of communication?
- Has there been a failure of management?
- Has there been a failure of technology?

Step 2: Communication

- Has everyone been informed who can help/needs to know (eg stakeholders and other interested parties – HR, marketing, PR, senior management and so forth)?
- Has the project team been brought up to date?
- Are communications honest and open?
- Is there a mechanism for feedback?
- Is there a clearly defined communication strategy?
- Are there clearly defined communications channels?

Step 3: Remedial action

The following points should be considered:

- Are the resources adequate?
- Are they the correct ones?
- Can the scope be reduced?
- Can the timetable be changed for the better?
- Can the project deliverables be phased to reduce pressure?
- Are there any lateral approaches that solve the problems in the short term?
- Will the effect of any remedial actions have too great a negative impact on the rest of the organization?
- Should the project be stopped?

Step 4: Follow-up

- Assuming things are getting better, are root causes being monitored?
- Is the effectiveness of the solution being checked against reality?
- Are there any symptoms of a new disaster in the offing?
- Keep asking 'What has changed?'
- Has the team/organization documented and learnt from the disaster?
- Have measures been put in place to keep things under control and on track?

If the reader takes nothing else away from this book, this checklist will help get a better outcome from a disaster. Please use it and feel free to adapt it based on experience and needs.

DIAGNOSTIC TOOL

When looking for the cause of a disaster, it can be useful to keep the number five in mind. This is helpful for two reasons. First, the five Ms are a good rule of thumb: Man (people), Machine (technology), Method (process), Material (structure), Milieu (environment). The causes of a failure will probably involve one or more of these. It is interesting to compare these with the five main causes given in Chapter 2. Figure 9.6 compares the two (there is an overlap in some cases).

Cause (five Ms)	Cause (Chapter 2)
Man	Unclear/wrong goals, failures of communication, failures of management
Machine	Unproven technology
Method	Failures of management, failures of communication
Material	Inadequate resources
Milieu	External events

Figure 9.6 Comparison of causes

Secondly, in Chapter 2, the case was made for multiple causes of a disaster; however, if it is suspected that there is a root cause, then it is helpful to try 'why' five times, as follows:

1. Why does A happen? Because of B.
2. Why does B happen? Because of C.
3. Why does C happen? Because of D.
4. Why does D happen? Because of E.
5. Why does E happen? Because of F. This is the 'root' cause.

This is an arbitrary number of questions, but the key point is 'don't take the first cause you come across as the only one, or the root one'. Although this is a useful diagnostic tool, the author's view is that there may well be multiple causes of a project failure; do not always expect to end up with just the one.

GIVING BAD NEWS – A USEFUL SKILL

The ability to give bad news to the team, or the client, is a vital skill for the project manager. The following advice was obtained from Suzy Siddons, an expert in communications. She advocates a three-step process for doing this. It needs to be applied slightly differently depending on the audience; in this case, teams and clients. First though, a recap on personal communications.

Communications cycle

Because communication is not as simple as many think, it is worthwhile to give a very brief overview of what happens in any person-to-person(s) communication. Keep this in mind before starting out to give bad news, or for that matter before any communications exercise (see Figure 9.7).

The key point here is that effective communication is not an accident; it requires thought and time. In a crisis where time is at a premium, it is very easy for communication to become offhand and thoughtless; this will only serve to make a bad situation worse and misunderstandings generate conflict within the team.

This is the basic three-step process (see Figure 9.8); it is assumed here that the audience is involved directly in the situation.

Note: Where bad news is being given to the press or an uninvolved third party, see also Chapter 6, PR.

To the team

In this case, the team is assumed to be made up of people, other than the end client, who are developing the deliverables for the project; it may include subcontractors and suppliers. The relationships with different parts of the team may vary, but the idea is that everyone is part of the same team.

The golden rule is 'do not hide anything from your team, but keep in mind that they may be hiding things from you.' As

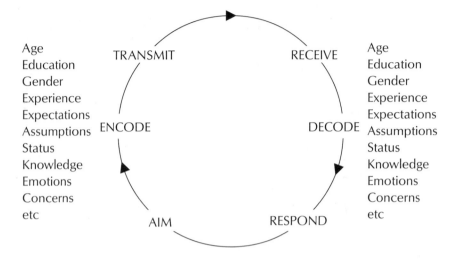

Figure 9.7 Communications cycle; the closer the match between the sender and the receiver, the easier the communication

Step	Description
1	Clearly state the situation, as it is perceived to be. Do not hide, embroider or play down the truth.
2	Ask if the audience has anything to add to what you have said, as they may know things you don't. Ask for any questions and give straightforward answers to the best of your knowledge.
3	What can we do now? As soon as possible start working towards a solution, a call for action.

Figure 9.8 Three-step process

discussed elsewhere in this book (for example in Chapter 4 on risk management), people often soften the bad news that they pass up the chain of command. This means that the project manager is likely to have knowledge gaps. Apart from the current crisis, there may be many minor, and not so minor, facts that need to be identified. Consequently, step three needs to be given plenty of attention.

Keep in mind the standard acronym for reacting to bad news, DABGA (denial, anger, bargaining, grief, acceptance). While this sequence is usually associated with serious trauma such as the death of a loved one, the stages apply to any sudden or serious bad news that a person may encounter. It will take time for the audience to come to terms with what has happened. So, the best strategy for the project manager is to take account of these stages and facilitate the team's progress through them. For example, consider setting up a discussion session, or a brain-storming event immediately after giving the bad news so that people can come to terms with matters. This also gives them something positive to do and provides a mechanism for the project manager to gather more information about what has actually happened.

To the client

The same general rules apply.

1. Tell it like it is, do not try to hide anything material or mislead the client.
2. Tell them what actions you have taken to put things right, identifying the problem.
3. Involve them in the solution, set realistic expectations.

The main difference is that the client may not be part of the team (though in joint-venture projects this may not be the case, in which case it is a judgement call as to what the exact situation is). However, as with the team, there is bound to be some element of 'DABGA' – at least the denial part – and it is important to allow people time to accept reality. Be prepared to let people take a break at this stage in the meeting for coffee or something to let the message sink in. Don't let them escape though; the last thing you want is for clients to go running off in a state of despair, spreading incomplete stories amongst all and sundry. Similarly, be prepared with all the relevant information that you think they may need and be ready to answer questions, some of which may be hostile.

Key point: When giving bad news to a client, it is important to be sure of the facts; going off 'half cocked' will lead to further problems. For example, if only a part of the problem has been identified and a solution found, then presenting this to the client with the suggestion that 'all will be well now' will lead to embarrassment when a 'new' problem occurs. A series of such events will rapidly erode the client's confidence in the project team. It is vital that the problem – there is seldom just one cause (see Chapter 2) – is properly identified and a complete solution offered. However, it should be acceptable to offer a way forward rather than a complete solution; it is a disaster that is being considered here, not a regular progress update.

Difficult situations/questions

It is, sadly, possible that the reaction to bad news can result in difficult situations or hostile questions. The best approach, with the most likely chance of a good outcome, is to adopt a 'win-win' strategy. Keep the following in mind when handling difficult situations after giving bad news:

- Don't interrupt.
- Talk about what has actually occurred, not what you think should have happened.
- Avoid any personal attacks or 'name calling'.
- Calmly ask for clarification if any of the points made are unclear.
- Don't make general statements – be as precise as possible.
- Allow all sides to put their case.
- Summarize at the end of each statement.
- Try to keep to the subject – extraneous matter should not be dragged in.
- Try not to use 'blaming' language; you are not looking at whose fault it is, just at what started the conflict.
- Look for positive outcomes.

- Any solutions should be reasonable and must look at what limits and restrictions exist.
- Try to be creative.
- Keep the idea that a solution is possible to the forefront.
- You are not making concessions – you are trying to solve a problem.
- Think of the consequences if the conflict is not resolved.
- Be fair.
- No 'dragging the body about' or recriminations.
- Be positive.
- Use realistic timescales.
- Keep a record of what has been agreed to do.
- Both sides must agree.

Another useful tool in question handling is STOP. First, you need to listen to the question all the way through, and then, before you answer:

- **S** Share the question (where appropriate) with the rest of the audience, who won't have heard it because they were all to busy thinking about the questions they wanted to ask.
- **T** Think about how you are going to answer the question.
- **O** Only answer the question – don't get side-tracked and don't go into too much detail
- **P** Politely check that your answer is OK.

This works and is short enough to be written on a cue card if you have a poor memory.

MOTIVATION

Motivation, or re-motivation, is another essential survival skill for the project manager. What is motivation? It is the force or process that causes people to act in a specific way. So, for example, hunger is the force that motivates us to seek food and eat it, or the processes of law motivate us to behave honestly. After the bad news that is associated with a disaster has been delivered, the members of the team are likely to require motivation. Suzy Siddons recommends the Expectancy Theory as being the most realistic model to adopt in an emergency where results are needed in a short time. In 1964, Victor Vroom working in conjunction with Edward Lawler and Lyman Porter suggested that the relationship between people's behaviour at work and their goals was not as simple as many thought. Vroom realized that an employee's performance is based on individual factors such as personality, skills, knowledge, experience and abilities. He said that you could motivate someone if they believe that:

- There is a positive correlation between efforts and performance.
- Favourable performance will result in a desirable reward.
- The reward will satisfy an important need.
- The desire to satisfy the need is strong enough to make the effort worthwhile.

Example: Maurice is taking his MBA at the Open University. He has a C+ average for the course and one more exam to do. He really wants to get a B for the course, and to do this he needs to get an A in the forthcoming exam. Maurice's motivation to study for this exam will be influenced by, first the expectation that hard work will lead to an A in the exam, and secondly, that getting an A in the exam will result in a B grade for the whole course.

If Maurice believes that he cannot get an A in the exam or that receiving an A will not lead to an overall grade of B for the course, he will not be motivated to study particularly hard.

A diagrammatic version of the application of Expectancy Theory is shown in Figure 9.9.

Effort > Performance (E>P) Expectancy Theory involves whether putting effort into a task will lead to high performance. This will depend on the individual's abilities, previous experience, tools,

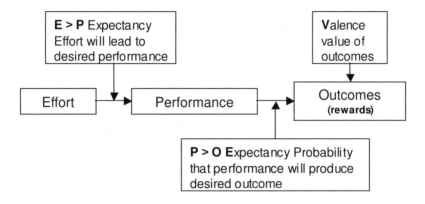

Figure 9.9 Application of Expectancy Theory

resources and opportunity to perform. If Maurice believes he can truly work hard enough to get an A, his E–P expectancy will be high and so will his motivation. If he doubts his ability, his E–P Expectancy will be low and so will his motivation to study.

Performance > Outcome (P>O) Expectancy Theory is about whether successful performance will be rewarded with the desired outcome. In Maurice's case, if he is assured by his tutor that an A in the exam will result in a B for the overall course, his P–O expectancy will be high and so will his motivation; but if he does not trust his tutor, or has reason to believe that an A will not get him what he wants, then his P–O expectancy will be low and he will not be motivated to study.

The final piece in the Expectancy Theory pattern is the *valence* or value that Maurice places on getting a B for the course. If he really doesn't care, the valence will be low and so will the motivation, but since he really wants to get a B, the valence is high and so is his motivation.

Note: For high motivation, all the factors E–P expectancy, P–O expectancy and valency of the outcome must be high.

Example: The same approach can be applied within a project team in the midst of a crisis. The project leader needs to make sure that the activities being requested fit with the requirements of this theory. It may be necessary for a team member to spend a long time working extra hours, looking at tedious detail and revisiting previous work to rectify a problem caused by someone else. This then needs to be related to an outcome, the successful rescue of the project, which will deliver a worthwhile result to the individual for the effort required. This may be a reward in the form of time off for a long weekend, a financial bonus, or a promise of promotion based on recognition of the commitment shown and so on.

Further information: Those wishing to know more about motivation in a team environment are referred to the following keywords as a starting point: Maslow's hierarchy of need, the ERG model, Hertzberg's two-factor theory, equity theory, and the acquired-need model.

Leadership

Closely related to motivation is leadership. Although this is not a book about leadership skills in general, in a disaster there are some critical leadership issues to keep in mind.

1. Remain calm at all times; set an example of being in control, even if you feel you are not.
2. Provide strong and positive leadership and keep the team informed.
3. Don't leave people with nothing to do; they will get bored and de-motivated.
4. Do not delegate blame or praise. It is important that the leader does this personally, and in private (particularly blame).
5. Do not allow public blaming or shaming; do not permit team members to assassinate each others' credibility.
6. Do listen to the team, as they are the ones with the actual knowledge of what is happening; involve them in decisions.

Key point: Remember that the strength of the team will support the individuals through the disaster; encouraging a cooperative approach will pay dividends. The role of the leader is to facilitate as well as to provide clear, and visible, direction for the team.

NEGOTIATION

Negotiation has often been useful in rescuing a project from disaster. There are many books available on the subject; for the purposes of this one, it is enough to say that negotiating on the basis of price, scope and timetable can provide a way forward.

Example: With a couple of weeks to go, it had finally been accepted that there was no way that the whole project could be delivered. The planned roll-out of replacement point-of-sales equipment to several hundred outlets could not be accomplished. Fortunately the client, though justifiably angry (and now losing trust in the supplier) at not being kept informed, was more interested in what could be done than what could not be done. Indeed, the client saw this as an opportunity to save money. Negotiations commenced, and a limited delivery, based on a phased roll-out region-by-region was agreed with a new time-table, at a reduced price to compensate the retail client.

There is a simple five-step life cycle that can be applied to negotiation: plan, explore, offer, barter, close. Figure 9.10 shows this negotiation cycle.

Plan: Identify what it is you want and then prioritize as high, medium and low priorities. The high-priority items are the things that you really must have, such as an absolute latest delivery date, a maximum price, minimum specification, etc. This is the bottom line below which you cannot go. The medium priority items are those that you would prefer to have but can survive without, possibly phased delivery and payment, or extended warranty terms. The low-priority items are those that you might like but are certainly not worth risking losing a must-have for. Examples include having the equipment painted in a particular colour or intellectual property rights for resale.

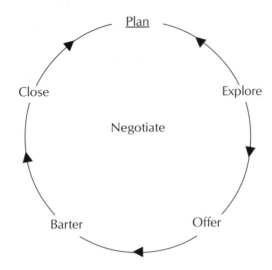

Figure 9.10 Five-step negotiation cycle

At this stage, you should also establish who you are negotiating with. In the case of third parties, this is complicated by the fact that there may be an intermediary between you and the client. You may be negotiating with the intermediary as well as the company for which you're to work, so you should try and define which parts of the deal affect which parties most. Typically, the third party is concerned with margin and cash flow rather than your customer. You may be dealing with the people who wish to use the equipment, but you have to get the order from a central purchasing department. The role of the people you negotiate with will have an effect on how they negotiate. This brings us to the concept of decision-makers and influencers.

Decision-makers: These are the people who actually make the decisions about the outcome of the negotiation, effectively the people who put their names on the cheque.

Influencers: These are the people who are involved in making the decision but do not take the responsibility for it. Typically, they are advisors, technical specialists, legal experts and so forth. It is important to establish that the person you are dealing with is the person who makes the decisions. For example, you may be having regular meetings with the people who will use the product you are selling once it has been purchased. However, it may be the finance manager who has to approve the spend. In this case, you will be dealing via the users of the systems as intermediaries, who will have the role of influencers but are not the decision-makers.

Explore: It is all too easy to miss this stage out and jump straight into the negotiations from the word go. This is a mistake; you will probably miss vital information for one thing, but also, by failing to get some sort of rapport going with the other person, increase the risk of misunderstanding their meaning. Once such mis-understandings are made, it is difficult to recover as your entire strategy will have been built on a falsehood.

When obtaining information, you should use 'open questions', essentially asking questions for which there is not a yes/no answer, encouraging the person to talk more freely and hence tell you what they think. You will often get pointers to further ques-tions you hadn't thought of. An example of an open question is 'What are the main problems that you get from your existing computer system?' However, once you have got all the informa-tion you think you need, you should always summarize what you have understood and gain agreement from the interviewee. This ensures that you are both negotiating about the same thing.

Offer: This is where the negotiation begins in earnest. Both parties will make their starting position clear; yours might be a monthly payment of £50, paid quarterly in arrears, on-site sup-port and a price review after 12 months; theirs might be £70 per month, payable in advance, fixed for 18 months with return-to-base support at your expense. It is important that you leave yourself room to manoeuvre; if your bottom line was £50 per month, then you should have not made it your opening bid. Similarly, you don't want to show all your bargaining counters up front; you need to keep them in reserve so you can make additional offers at a later stage. You can introduce them using the 'if. . ., then' technique, where you make acceptance of one point conditional upon accepting another.

Barter: The nitty-gritty part of the negotiation and how you handle matters here will profoundly affect the outcome of the process. The key point here is never to give anything away without getting something back in return.

Close: The end. You have agreed a deal and defined what the terms and conditions are going to be. As stated in 'Explore', it is vital that all involved are sure that they have the same understanding as to what has been agreed. It is essential that this is written down and that what is written is agreed as binding. Whilst this is being done, it is a good idea to reinforce the benefits that you are all getting from the deal and be prepared to be firm should it seem that negotiations are about to restart.

SUMMARY

This chapter has been all about what can be done to alleviate the impact of a disaster. The strategies, recipes and skills described have all been known to work and are worthy of consideration. The very act of considering them implies that the project team is taking time to see the wood despite the trees. Identifying what the real problems are and choosing a suitable strategy is the first step towards dealing with a project disaster. The next step is implementing the strategy and then putting in place the necessary safeguards to stop a new disaster springing up – hence the need to find root causes.

CHECKLIST

Answer the questions for your project presented in Figure 9.11 and take corrective action as needed. If you are dealing with a disaster and don't understand the corrective action that will be required, get help from someone who does. You may not have time to learn the relevant skills yourself, but at least you now know the area of ignorance; this is step one to resolving the problem.

Question/comment	Yes/no?
Which of these is being considered/has been done: – doing nothing? – starting from scratch? – admit defeat? – review and continue?	
Has the sample method been tried by: – identifying causes? – communication? – taking remedial action? – following up?	
Has the 'five Ms' tool been applied (Man, Machine, Method, Material, Milieu)?	
When giving bad news have you: – clearly stated the situation and not hidden anything from the team? – asked the audience for their information/questions? – made a call for action?	
When answering questions do you STOP? – **S**hare the question by repeating? – **T**hink about how you will answer? – **O**nly answer the question – don't side-track (or 'rat-hole') – **P**olitely check your answer is understood/OK?	
Has the team been (re-)motivated using an appropriate combination of effort/performance/outcome?	
Is positive leadership being shown?	
When negotiating do you: – plan, prioritizing what you wish to achieve? – identify who the decision-makers/influencers are and what are their needs? – explore options available? – offer based on a starting position (with a clear 'bottom line' in mind)? – barter, giving nothing away without something in return? – close, confirming and documenting the agreed deal?	

Figure 9.11 Checklist: Recipes and skills

10

What not to do

Up to now, this book has dealt with causes, cures and survival strategies. In this chapter, the emphasis is on the negative. These are the strategies and approaches that people have taken that have been shown to fail. Of course, that does not mean they will always fail, but their track record to date is not encouraging and before embarking on any of them, think at least twice. There is often a better, less risky, strategy available, and it is worth taking the time to think about this before following any of these negative approaches. These negative strategies include: do nothing; lie about it; resign; break the contract; throw more resources at it, blame the subcontractors; and blame the client. Choose carefully.

DO NOTHING

What the strategy is

The 'do nothing' strategy involves masterly inactivity: carry on regardless with the project team attempting the activities as planned and hope it all comes right in the end. This is the equivalent of 'something will turn up'. There is a saying about rearranging the deck chairs on the *Titanic*. This strategy is just sitting in them and admiring the view of the iceberg.

Why this is attractive

It is closely linked with the concept of denial; doing nothing allows the project team, and higher management, to believe that all will be well in the end. Senior management may or may not be aware that this strategy is being adopted, but if they are not aware then it says much about the way they do their job. Everyone can carry on as if all is well with the world. It saves the project manager from having to give unwelcome news to the bosses. The author remembers one extreme example where the account manager decided to leave passing on bad news to the client until after he had been on holiday. The hope was that it would all be magically fixed by the time he got back. It wasn't – it was worse and he now also had to explain why he had kept quiet.

It is also attractive, at least in the short term, because it allows thinking time. 'We know we are in a mess, but let's keep going whilst we think of a better solution – at least we will look as though something is still being achieved.' Routine activity is soothing and can serve as a welcome distraction from reality.

Why it is dangerous

The 'do nothing' strategy is dangerous because it delays acceptance of the inevitable and consequently delays the time before corrective action is taken. In some cases, the disasters would never have developed to the point of total irrevocability if they had been accepted just a few days earlier. The longer problems are ignored, the harder it becomes to fix them. This applies to almost every aspect of recovery. For example, if the primary cause of a disaster is having the wrong resources, then no amount of time spent waiting will fix this. Worse, by not taking action that perhaps requires management/HR support, there may never be a chance to get the right resources.

In addition, it is likely that members of the project team will know what the real situation is. This has two potential impacts: first, that the team will become disillusioned and lose confidence in the project/manager, and secondly, that word will get out and embarrassing questions will be asked – adding to the problems.

Has it ever worked?

The author knows of one case where it did. This was a project for a large telecommunications company that was investigating possibilities for utility meter reading via spare capacity in telephone lines. A critical small sub-project, which had a project team of only three, had the misfortune to lose all three team members for overlapping and extended times. The slippage on the sub-project was in excess of 100 per cent. However, the telecommunications company's delays were far greater, so that although technically this was a disaster, doing nothing did not cause any problems.

Not having recourse to sufficient information, it is not possible to say whether this strategy has worked other than rarely. The example given is the only one the author knows about, but 'do nothing' is always an option considered in any management consultancy report, though the reason for this is usually to allow for the 'if it ain't broke, don't fix it' option. In the case of a project disaster, this is unlikely to be so. It almost certainly is 'broke'.

Note: During the editorial phase of this book, an alternative view of this strategy was offered to the author. Doing nothing can avoid making things worse. There is an analogy here with the medical dictum that goes roughly 'if in doubt, do no harm'. This was considered to be useful if the project disaster had just been 'dumped' on the manager concerned – a valid point of view, but within the context of this book a disaster is something that is happening rather quickly. Sitting back and doing nothing is unlikely to be helpful – you would not expect an airline pilot to sit there waiting to see if the fire goes out or the engines restart themselves. Action will normally be required.

BE ECONOMICAL WITH THE TRUTH (LIE)

What the strategy is

Usually, this means telling the world outside of the project (or sponsoring organization) 'problem, what problem?' and hoping that it can be fixed before it can no longer be hidden and the truth gets out. It can also mean deceiving members of the project team itself – though they normally have a good idea of what is actually going on. It can also mean the project staff not being prepared to 'whistle blow'.

Example: With less than 60 days to go, the senior members of the project team were summoned to a meeting with a senior member of the customer's team. The customer asked 'Are we going to meet the deadline?' Those present looked from one to another, and finally to their boss. The boss said nothing, so, thinking about their career prospects, the team members said nothing either. In fact, several of them knew perfectly well that the project had little chance of being delivered on time, and had told their boss so many times. The project ended up as a disaster in most senses of the word.

Why this is attractive

This is largely because it takes the immediate heat off the project team or the organization and provides breathing space. Sometimes it is done to avoid simple loss of face. The hope is normally that the issues can be solved before the truth has a chance to escape to a wider audience (normally the client). As described in

Chapter 6 on PR, this is not a good strategy, as being caught out will usually destroy the working relationship.

It can happen that the team thinks it can fix the problem in the near future and that there is no harm in keeping quiet about something that the client need never become aware of. 'All's well that ends well' is the driving philosophy here.

Why it is dangerous

As with doing nothing, the trouble comes from the delay in accepting reality. This can show itself in many ways. For example, a funding crisis cannot be solved if nobody outside of the team knows it exists; eg there may be insufficient budget left to pay for the staff needed to deploy the equipment to the client's business premises. It is possible that everything may be made to work but that it is then impossible for the customer to receive the end result. If the budget shortfall was made clear, it might have been possible to renegotiate or to look at other options.

It is also bad news because once the truth is revealed, those who have concealed it can never regain any credibility. After this has happened, the only way forward is to remove all those involved from the scene. Typically, the client will do this for you by, at best, taking their business elsewhere, or worse, entering into punitive litigation. Experience shows that with most clients it is better to give bad news, together with an honest plan of how you are going to correct it, than to have them find out later.

Note: The author notes that there are some clients, and the late Robert Maxwell was a case in point, who are so irrational that doubt may be cast over the case for openness and honesty. Such people see honesty as a weakness and an opportunity to renegotiate, or just as an excuse to show off/have a temper tantrum. Fortunately, such psychopathic clients are fairly rare.

Has it ever worked?

Rarely, if ever, has this strategy worked; the truth will always come out. However, in political cases (with a capital P), enquiries and redefinitions have been deployed to demonstrate that black is white. For the purposes of this book, such semantic exercises which result in failure being presented as success don't count. It is usually better to say what is going to be done to rescue the situation than to pretend it doesn't exist.

ABANDON SHIP/RESIGN

What the strategy is

The project manager and/or the appropriate senior manager is removed from the scene, or possibly the organization. In extreme cases, it happens very suddenly, within minutes of the decision being made.

Why this is attractive

The abandon ship/resign strategy is attractive because, by getting rid of a figurehead/person or persons who can be blamed, a sacrificial victim is provided. This demonstrates to the client that something is being done. It also can be used to support a case that 'now we have a new team, things will be fine'. It also provides a punctuation mark in the project that can be used to buy time, find a solution, renegotiate and so on.

It can also provide a welcome escape route for the 'victim'. The author has seen this happen at least once where an individual was moved sideways (arguably promoted) into a new role and the client was provided with a new manager. This new manager was therefore provided with a nearly clean slate to restart the relationship. This worked well for a while; sadly, the real cause of the disaster was not the project manager alone, and in the longer term the more fundamental flaws resurfaced.

Why it is dangerous

To start with, getting rid of the project/programme manager (or whoever) is unlikely to be the solution to the problem, even if they were bad at their job. It is only likely to make matters better in the long run if additional action is taken to deal with the real reasons for the disaster. If badly handled, there can be a negative impact on the morale of the remaining members of the project team, and possibly the organization as a whole. Furthermore, bringing in new management to the team will inevitably mean that the team has to go through a new 'forming' stage in team-building (see Appendix 1, 'Teams') and its productivity will be degraded. However, as the project is already a disaster, its rescue is unlikely to be overnight whatever strategy is adopted; this may be a price worth paying.

Has it ever worked?

It has certainly bought time for projects. It has certainly allowed the poison to be drawn from a bad working relationship. However, as discussed in Chapter 2, 'Why project disasters happen', there is seldom a single cause of a project disaster, and the causes will probably still remain. It also panders to the modern blame culture that is not well known for solving problems. Making it someone's fault does not turn bad into good.

Example: Although not a project, this strategy was employed by the BBC in the case of the great Hutton enquiry/Alastair Campbell dispute between the BBC and the New Labour Government relating to the Iraq war. Greg Dyke, the Director General of the BBC, together with a number of other senior figures was forced to resign. The BBC continues; its independent survival was threatened.

BREAK THE CONTRACT

What the strategy is

Quite simply, this involves putting a halt to the project and letting the lawyers get on with it. The client is informed that, for the price quoted, it is not possible to deliver the goods. Note that this does not mean that a small or even a moderate-to-large loss would be made in delivering what was required. It means that the consequences for the organization would be devastating if the project were to be allowed to continue.

Why this is attractive

It isn't really! However, it can be an effective last resort when the alternative is to carry on with an irretrievable failure. It gives a relatively clean break and will allow many team members and other resources to move on or be redeployed to better effect. There may be a spin-off benefit in improving the morale of these people; they may even be able to help other projects to achieve real benefits for the organization.

Why it is dangerous

Breaking a contractual obligation is not something to be entered into lightly. The only people who are certain to win will be the lawyers, who will doubtless collect sizeable fees. Even if it gets the organization out of the immediate disaster, it will certainly stretch, and more likely break, the relationship with the client. New business with the client is unlikely in the near future. Furthermore, it will not leave those who worked on the project feeling motivated; some will probably leave, and overall morale will be damaged. The organization's reputation will also be adversely affected. All in all, there is little good to come from this other than escape from the immediate impact of the disaster.

Has it ever worked?

Actually, it has been known to work as a last line of defence. In one case, a project to develop a support service for a large supermarket chain resulted in success, in so far as the service worked, but in disaster in that the incurred and ongoing costs resulting from the project were insupportable. It was cheaper to abandon the whole project, pay penalties and lose the client than to have continued (which could have led to bankruptcy for the organization concerned in the longer term).

Note: Always get good legal advice before breaking any legally binding contract.

THROW MORE RESOURCES AT IT

What the strategy is

Quite simply, this involves applying more money, people, and machinery to the problem, the reasoning being that if something isn't going to be finished on time with 20 people, then adding an extra 20 should get things done more quickly. The same rationale can be applied to equipment and money.

Why this is attractive

There are three main reasons for this. First, visibility; it makes it clear that something is being done about solving the problem. Secondly, leadership; resources are being mobilized, the problem is being highlighted and action is being taken. Thirdly, there is a mistaken belief that it will solve any problem.

Why it is dangerous

To start with, it is based on a false premise. The old chestnut that if 2 people can dig a hole in 4 hours, then 48 people can dig the same hole in 10 minutes, gives the problem away. There just isn't room in the hole for 24 people at the same time. In more sophisticated terms, there is all the business of team dynamics, team-building, briefing, training and so forth, but the basic concept holds true. Crudely throwing resources blindly at a problem won't help.

Next the resource – financial, people or equipment – has to come from somewhere, and it is always in finite supply. Even were it to solve the project's problem (improbable for reasons already given), it is very likely to cause knock-on effects elsewhere in the organization which could well kick off many new disasters.

Finally, the consequences in terms of escalating costs (for little or even negative benefit) and reduced morale of an even greater number when it fails, will risk turning a disaster into a catastrophe.

Has it ever worked?

In the case where the driving reason for the project disaster was insufficient resources/funding, then this should improve things. Indeed, that is the best solution for helping an under-resourced project, providing the resource is the correct one and introduced in a controlled manner. However, it may not be the instant fix that some might expect – it will take time to get people briefed, equipment in place and working effectively. There will be disruption to the project team. In the short term, adding more resources will often reduce productivity whilst things settle down. Thereafter, things should get better. So yes, it can and has been seen to work. However, in the case where the cause of the problem is simply the wrong resource or something else altogether, such as false assumptions, unclear goals or the wrong project in the first place, then it will not help. There are many examples where this approach has made matters worse. This approach is less common than it was in the 1970s and 1980s (when it was a relatively common strategy), but it still has its followers because it is an easy option.

BLAME THE SUBCONTRACTORS

What the strategy is

Rather than admitting that your organization has made any errors, this strategy involves blaming the suppliers/subcontractors for failing to deliver (see also the section on being economical with the truth, if they have not failed to deliver).

Why this is attractive

The 'blame the subcontractors' strategy is attractive because it allows the use of the excuse 'beyond our reasonable control'. It passes the buck to someone else and gets the prime contractor off the hook. At least that is the idea. Of course, it may well be the case that the subcontractors have failed to deliver, but that is unlikely to be the whole story.

Why it is dangerous

This is a dangerous strategy because managing subcontractors is part of the job of the project team. It may be reasonable to expect the customer to accept that subcontractor delays can result in project delays. But remember that this book is dealing only with situations that are disastrous. If that is the case, and the project manager has not seen the problem coming and taken mitigating action, then something was very wrong somewhere.

Has it ever worked?

This is unknown to the author; it has certainly been seen to be used many times as a negotiation technique to buy time. However, it is unlikely to get an organization out of a real disaster, as the management of suppliers is the prime contractor's responsibility.

BLAME THE CLIENT

What the strategy is

This is a variation on blaming the subcontractor. The disaster is their fault, not yours. The client has failed to meet their obligations, changed their mind, behaved unreasonably, not paid on time and so on. The idea is to escape with an unstained reputation and hopefully still get paid enough to make it worthwhile.

Why this is attractive

It is attractive because, if it works, then the disaster is not the fault of the project manager or the organization. It avoids blame and, hopefully, leaves the impression that everything was done professionally. The disaster was beyond reasonable control and could not have been avoided. It also allows the project team to feel that it did a good job, and so morale should not suffer too much. Finally, it leaves the reputation of the organization intact, and so should not adversely impact the chances of wining new business with other prospective clients.

Why it is dangerous

The strategy of blaming the client is dangerous because 'the customer is always right, even when wrong'. Supplier organizations seldom come off well by blaming their clients. There have been some very public rows where large-scale outsourcing suppliers to the UK Government have blamed all the faults and problems on the client. The long-term effect of this on at least one such organization has been a substantial reduction in Government business in the UK. Organizations that end up at loggerheads with their clients seldom come out of it unscathed. Given a choice, would you go for the organization that had a poor track record of blaming its clients or for the one where relations were good? This strategy is potentially bad for the organization's image and brand.

Again, as with blaming the subcontractor, it can be argued that managing the client is also part of the role of the project management or account team. If the team has allowed scope (sometimes known as mission) creep to go on uncontrolled, or has failed to monitor or control change, then this is really not the client's direct fault (see also Chapter 2, which considers uncontrolled change as an augury of impending doom).

Has it ever worked?

Yes, but only when the client has been blatantly, and publicly, unreasonable. A case study mentioned earlier covers this situation. Just before the project was due to deliver a live service, the client cancelled the entire programme, their reason being that they had 'revalidated the business case and no longer felt the project worthwhile'. It seemed a little late for the client to be deciding on the business case for a large programme (the example involved many millions of pounds) and the reality was probably political – a new director did not like the supplier organization. As can be imagined, this made some money for the legal profession before a compromise was reached, and some of the supplier's costs were covered.

SUMMARY

Every business book needs a summary, and this one is no exception. The goal has been to identify why disasters happen and to suggest what can be done to survive them with the best possible outcome. The causes and strategies discussed have all been based on real experiences of people working on real projects. Using the right strategies has been shown to get the best possible outcome from a project disaster. Learning from disasters will help avoid them in the future – those who do not learn from history are doomed to repeat the same mistakes. Some go further and suggest that it is possible to remove the majority of causes of disaster by following the correct, knowledge-based, approach. Whatever happens, the author is convinced that there will continue to be project disasters, particularly in any high-technology environment. Consequently, it is hoped that this book will continue to be of help to project workers for a long time to come. Good luck.

CHECKLIST

Answer the questions presented in Figure 10.1 for your project and take corrective action as needed. If you are dealing with a disaster, and don't understand the corrective action that will be required, get help from someone who does. You may not have time to learn the relevant skills yourself, but at least you now know the area of ignorance; this is step one to resolving the problem.

Question/comment	Yes/no?
Doing nothing? – Is this deliberate, ie doing no harm whilst assessing the situation? – Are you waiting to see if matters change because of events external to the project? – If by default, then assess the situation and take action instead.	
Lying about the situation? – Is this helpful? – Will the situation definitely be resolved before the lie is exposed? – Are you confident that you have not been lied to? – Are you really sure you want to adopt this very high-risk strategy?	
Abandoning ship? – Will your removal/sacrifice benefit the project? – Is there someone better qualified available to take over? – Will the turbulence caused by the change in leadership be too great?	
Breaking the contract? – Are there valid grounds for doing this (eg client action)? – What will the repercussions be? – Has appropriate legal advice been obtained? – Are you happy to lose the client?	
Blindly throwing resources at the problem? – Does the project need more resources? – Are the new resources the correct ones for the job? – Are the current resources being deployed to best advantage? – Would new resources be available in time?	
Blaming the client or subcontractors? – Are they genuinely to blame? – Even if they are, is blaming helping the situation? – What specific gains are envisaged? – Would it be more helpful to negotiate using 'fault' as a bargaining counter?	

Figure 10.1 Checklist: What not to do

Appendix 1: Teams

Inevitably, teams are part and parcel of projects. Consequently, anyone in the midst of an ongoing disaster needs some basic understanding of factors affecting team performance. This appendix covers the project life cycle, and how projects fit into the larger picture. These need to be looked at when in the midst of chaos in order to find out where you are and what you should be doing about it. This information is provided as a starting point – but it may be all the reader has time for.

LIFE-CYCLE

Team formation

When a group of people form a team, they go through a series of behaviours that help to form the team into a working unit. These stages always occur when the team members are new to each other and the project. There are three basic stages that the team must go through before they can begin to perform.

Forming

When a group of strangers first come together, they desperately need to know what they are there for. They have a head full of unanswered questions that concern them:

'Why am I here?' 'What are we expected to do?' 'How long is this going to take?' 'What are our objectives?'

This is the 'forming' stage in team development, and until every person knows what they are there for, both as individuals and as a group, they simply will not get down to any work. The project manager's main responsibility at this point is to ensure that clear objectives are set, talked through and agreed, both verbally and in writing.

Anything that helps to identify the team with the project is useful at this point. It may seem a small point, but very often a project team name can help with this process. Some of the most effective project teams the author has worked with not only had a name, but also a logo, which identified everything that the team produced; they also had a slogan or mission statement that clearly stated what they were trying to achieve.

Lack of direction at this point is lethal. The 'forming' stage is rather like the start of a relay race, where every participant needs to know where the start and finish line are and what the rules are that control the race's smooth running. Imagine the chaos if this information wasn't given to all the participants before they started.

Storming

Now that the project's objectives and goals have been set, the members of the team begin to ask another set of questions:

'Who is in charge here?' 'What is my status in the team?' 'Who else is in the team?'

This is the 'storming' stage in team development, where each member begins to mark out their own position within the team. The project manager needs, at this point, to make sure that the team gets to know what each person is going to do, who reports to whom and what is expected of each other. People have a natural need to not only test out their position within the team, but also to tell the rest of the team something about themselves and their background. The project manager can help with this process by introducing each team member in turn to the group and telling the team why each person is involved with the project.

Often at this point there may be a challenge to the project leader from one or more members of the newly formed team. This may seem uncomfortable for the leader, but it is an important testing of both the project leader's ability to control events and the need for powerful personalities to make their mark on the proceedings. A wise project manager will handle any such challenge with diplomacy and firmness, bearing in mind that what the team needs at this point is strong leadership and direction, while understanding the reasons for the challenge.

Norming

The team is coming together at this point, but there is still one further stage that needs to take place. This is the 'norming' stage, where the team, often quite spontaneously, begins to produce a set of spoken and unspoken rules about the way they will work together. Some of these norms are quite specific: for instance, how often they will meet, how they will communicate with each other and the leader, and how often they will communicate. Other norms are more personal: things like how much information the team might wish to disclose (whether they share personal information), how formal or informal they will be, how they dress, how punctual they will be, how enthusiastic they are about their tasks and so on. These norms make the team feel comfortable and give the team a unique identity. The norms represent the face that the team presents to the world. If any team member refuses to abide by these norms, the team will often subtly edge the dissenting member out. Team norms may take a little time to develop (usually by the third or fourth team meeting they will be established), but they are an essential part of the team's smooth functioning.

Communication needs

The communication needs of a team at each stage are very clear. In the 'forming' stage, objectives must be set, discussed and accepted. Individual task areas need to be defined and agreed, timescales need to be set and standards must be clearly understood. This should be done both verbally and in writing. Whoever is leader at this point does not need to spend time making friends – this is not what the team needs at this moment. What is needed is clear direction, clear tasking and clear organization. The logistics of team meetings and communication standards need to be set up at this point as well, with answers to a number of questions. Where shall they meet? When? How often? How will they communicate? What is the team called? Who are they responsible to as a team? What resources do they have at their disposal?

Once the team members know where they are going, they start to ask questions like 'Who is leader here? What is my position within the team? What is my status here?' The 'storming' stage can be uncomfortable, with people jostling for position and often challenging the person who is seen as the leader at the beginning of the team's formation. Again, this is quite natural, and until individuals know and are satisfied with their position within the team, they will not move forward as a team members.

At this stage, the communication needs of the team are also clear – they must be able to discuss and express themselves. The team leader at this point should act as umpire and chairperson, and should be available for consultation and mediation, but must not be too directive or autocratic, as otherwise the team will probably turn on him or her and fight!

At the 'norming' stage, the unspoken and unwritten rules that the team uses to keep itself together and feeling comfortable are thrashed out. These may be things like the sort of clothes they wear, whether the team is punctual or unpunctual, how they address each other, whether they all go out for a drink after work, how much people tell each other about their personal life, how formal or informal they are at meetings, how much information is shared, etc. This is not over until the team feels that each of them knows how to behave and agrees with those behaviours. Indeed, team norms are sometimes so strong that if an individual member refuses to abide by them, then the team may well expel that individual.

At this point, the leader should be a participant rather than a dictator. It is generally true that the leader's behaviour will influence the team (for instance, if the leader is punctual, the team is usually punctual; if the leader is rude to team members, the team will be rude to each other and the leader; and so on); but it is the team that is ultimately the creator of norms rather than the leader.

After a team has 'formed', 'stormed' and 'normed', then, and only then, can the team move on to the most successful stage of team behaviour – performing.

Group think – a cure

In the body of the book the problem of Group Think in successful teams was identified – potentially leading to a disaster, if caught early it can be cured. Simply make sure that there is someone acting as a devil's advocate, and that rigorous examination of alternatives continues, the Project Manager needs to check that those taking the opponent or outsider roles are not being ignored and a healthy scepticism about "everything going smoothly" should be fostered.

Change

From the point of view of someone trying to cope with a project disaster, it is a fact that any change to a team kicks off the whole 'forming, storming, norming' process again.

Team dynamics

Another area for project managers to be aware of is that of team dynamics. Figure A1.1 shows the basic dynamics.

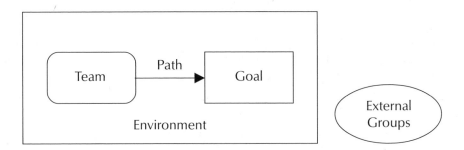

Figure A1.1 Basic team dynamics

Team: Who you work with. Factors to consider include: size, maturity, skill set, personalities, roles within the team, leadership style, experience of team members, expectations, motivation and reward.

Goal: The team's objective (remember SMART), how it is defined, timescales, how each team member is to contribute to achieving the goal, etc.

Path: Methods used to achieve the goal, who does what, use of internal and external resources, motivation process, reporting and delegation processes, etc.

Environment: The world in which the team operates, the department, division, etc. of the company, politics, standards, shared resources, attitude of people outside the team to the project, desk space, computer resources, effect of goals on this environment, etc.

External groups: Other groups that may affect the team, groups that have goals that conflict with the team's, groups that have staff seconded to the team, groups that compete for the same resources, etc.

If this is unfamiliar, then it may be that you have been put in a role that you need help to complete. Ask.

SUMMARY

Working in a project environment inevitably means working in teams. Knowing how teams work is essential if you are going to be a really effective team manager or member. It is important to understand what happens when people join or leave a team (having an induction pack for the project, detailing key points and where the coffee machine is can help here) and the effect it will have on performance. Knowing how the project environment interacts with the rest of the world provides an important perspective, particularly when things are going wrong. Topics for further research (see the Bibliography) include team roles, personal working styles, personal profiles and so forth. There may not be time to learn such things during a disaster, but it can help for next time.

Appendix 2: Stress

When a project has reached the critical list and a disaster is about to happen, or has already happened, then it is likely that the individuals involved will become stressed. It is important to be able to recognize the symptoms of stress, as people who are stressed-out become much less effective. It is also very unhealthy for those suffering from stress, and it is inexcusable to ignore their well-being. This appendix looks at the signs that indicate stress and suggests courses of action. Keep in mind that this book is not a medical text and no medical advice is offered, but knowing something about the subject is useful for those experiencing a disaster. Because the author is not an expert in this field, what follows is based on advice from Suzy Siddons, literature research and interviews with managers.

WHAT IS IT?

Stress is what happens when someone is put in a situation where they are under the wrong amount of pressure. The idea is that for each individual, there is an ideal level of pressure – demands made upon them – which will get the best results. Too great a demand and people struggle and find it difficult to cope – they are stressed. Too little and they get bored and fractious; again they are stressed. It is a little like Goldilocks and the Three Bears – it needs to be 'just right'.

When people are stressed, then the fight/flight response is kicked off, but the office environment does not provide an outlet for this – this can lead to both physiological and mental damage. Stress is not a good thing!

Example: The author had the misfortune to work, briefly, for a small organization where the proprietors bullied the permanent staff and were always shouting at them and berating them. These people were always stressed-out, and the working environment was both unpleasant and unproductive as a result. It was noticeable that there was a fairly high level of absence through sickness. In this case, the only solution available to those who worked there to escape this stress was to leave. This is an extreme example, but it is included to make the point that there may not be a solution to stress within the remit of the project manager.

CAUSES

Different things cause stress in different people. What may wind up one person, has no effect on another. For example, the author and his wife recently discovered that they are what in the United States are known as 'control freaks'. This cause of stress was discovered during a wedding where the timetable and locations for the various events were not made clear until just before they were due to happen. This was not because they had not been planned, but because they had not been communicated. As a result, everything seemed to be happening at the last minute, and the comfort of understanding the overall plan of the weekend was missing. By the end of the festivities, both were completely stressed-out and really happy to be on the aircraft home – this had a scheduled take-off time and a predicted destination.

Typical causes of stress include:

- unreasonable demands on timetable;
- impossible workloads;
- boredom;

- environmental factors such as noise, poor lighting, heat and cold, and so forth;
- conflicting priorities, such as home vs work;
- confusion, poor communication of what is required;
- inconsistent messages from managers – what is good today is bad tomorrow;
- being asked to perform tasks but not being trained to do them;
- being over- or under-stimulated;
- conflicts between individuals.

The causes of stress boil down to unreasonable pressures on the individual. These will vary from person to person.

Note: An approaching deadline can be either a cause of stress or a positive stimulus to succeed; it depends on the person and the circumstances.

SIGNS OF STRESS

People behave differently when under stress – there is no single specific indication that shows when one person is more stressed than they were before. Rather, it is change in behaviour, emotional state, mental processes or physical responses that provide the clue that something is not quite right.

In yourself

- *Behavioural* clues – when people are stressed, their behaviour is prone to change. Typically, they become curt, tempers shorten and voices are raised. They can also become more 'active', displaying fidgety gestures and unusual physical activity. On the other hand, they can become withdrawn and uncommunicative. The key point here is change. If you are normally bad tempered, then becoming quiet may be an indicator of stress.
- *Emotional* clues – feeling more depressed than usual, possibly feeling very elated, specific feelings of panic or guilt.

- *Mental* clues – it becomes hard to prioritize, there is increased difficulty in making decisions, inability to concentrate or becoming overly focused on one activity to the exclusion of all others.
- *Physical* changes – stress can result in actual physiological signs. Headaches, digestive problems, stiffening neck and shoulder muscles, conditions such as eczema, rashes and asthma can be worsened. Sleep disturbance is extremely common – usually shown by either an inability to sleep deeply or waking up and worrying.

To recognize such symptoms in yourself, you need to be able to identify changes from your 'normal' state. It can be helpful to recall how you reacted in similar situations in the past. Is your reaction more extreme? You can also talk to close friends and family to see if they recognize changes.

In others

As with recognizing stress in yourself, it is generally thought that stress in others shows itself in four areas – behaviourally, mentally, physically and emotionally. The difference is that when it is you, you know how you feel, your physical condition, what you think about and so forth. With others, you need to look for signs. Expect the symptoms to be as described above, but accept that they will be more difficult to observe, particularly in people you do not know well.

Example: The author was called in to help with a sales proposal that was at a critical stage. On arrival for the first day, the person for whom the work was to be done just sat in front of their computer screen for the first two hours without saying anything. The individual had 'tunnel vision' and could not get away from the task at hand to brief or to delegate.

EFFECTS OF STRESS ON EFFICIENCY

It is not necessary to go into any great lengths here: stress is bad news for both individuals and teams. There is a myth that people work better under stress, and there is much rubbish talked by people who boast 'I thrive on stress.' Stress means that the load placed on the individual or team is outside tolerable limits. In such circumstances, performance is always reduced, which will in turn tend to add to the overall stress in a downward spiral of performance. Goals and deadlines can be positive and energizing, but they should not be confused with stress.

STRESS AS A CAUSAL FACTOR IN A DISASTER

Once a key project team member or even the whole team becomes stressed, then it is easy for a vicious circle to develop where matters will get further and further out of hand and stress levels will increase. This can even be to the point where an individual breaks down and is unable to function within the project in question. If there is evidence of unusual levels of stress within a troubled project, then getting this down to a 'healthy' level can only be helpful.

WHAT TO DO ABOUT IT

First of all, don't fall into the 'I can fix it for everyone' trap. It can be tempting to try and take away the causes of stress for individuals. This can easily result in the stress simply being passed on to the manager, who then proceeds to collapse under the strain. Also keep in mind that, as in the example given in the Introduction, there are some circumstances where it is not possible for the project manager, or any team member, to do anything about the situation.

Example: Project members are having difficulty keeping their plans and reports up to date. The manager takes on board this work, just questioning people to get the basic data, then doing the work him- or herself. The team members are having difficulty dealing with the client's staff; the manager takes on this role.

This doesn't actually work for two reasons. First, if you remove all the burdens and pressures, then people feel that they are no longer contributing and they get bored – another cause of stress in itself. Second, the end result will be that by taking on the burdens you get stressed instead. Given that a project disaster is going on, then this extra stress could well push you over the edge – not a useful outcome. Just moving the problems on does not solve the real problem. Taken at an extreme, you end up with a bored, stressed team and an over-stretched, stressed project manager. Everyone loses.

A better way is to get people working at a point where there is enough pressure (or stress) to drive them on, but not so much that they can't cope.

A recipe

A simple recipe for this follows a four-stage process (based on a model presented in *Pressure at Work: A Survival Guide* by Tanya Arroba and Kim James). This four-stage process may be summarized as follows:

1. Make contact

Talk to the stressed-out team member; if they haven't come to you, go to them. Ordinarily, this is considered to be something to be done with great care, and that really the manager should be engendering a working environment where this can happen more easily. However, this is a project disaster under consideration; waiting for the right time or engineering the right moment is often not an option. Of course, if you, the project manager, are the cause of the problem, then this won't work!

- Use open questions and observations to initiate discussion.
- Keep away from judgemental statements.
- Adopt a relaxed and open posture.

2. Explore

- Use active listening, be receptive.
- Use open questions.
- Focus the discussion and summarize.

3. Understand

- Offer new perspectives, propose alternatives.
- Interpret.
- Confront identified problems.
- Encourage lateral thinking to find solutions.

4. Decide

- Employ decision-making skills to help reach a conclusion.
- Identify resources available to help.

Note: There are a wide range of personal skills needed to deal with stress in individuals or teams. These include active listening, asking open questions, coaching, assertion and so on. As has been said before, in a project disaster there is unlikely to be time to gain new skills quickly enough to be effective. Hopefully, the limited awareness of stress and dealing with it presented here will point the project manager in the right direction. If nothing else, if he or she can identify the problem, then it becomes possible to go elsewhere to seek appropriate help.

Remove the cause

A simple solution, but not always easy to adopt, is to remove the cause of the stress. If people are tired, then get them to take a break (for example, most experts consider that regular breaks should be taken from working at a computer screen; there are even Health and Safety regulations relating to this). If people are drowning in the sheer volume of work required, then look at getting additional resources. If the office is too cold, get a heater, and so forth. Where there is a simple solution, then use it.

Case study: A bid team was struggling to define the solution that was to be proposed to the client. There were only a few days to go before the proposal needed to be signed off and people had been working through the night, not taking proper meal breaks and generally putting in too many hours. Consequently, mistakes were being made, and many hours of work were being wasted. In one case, an error in the design of the IT infrastructure meant that a complicated pricing spread-sheet had to be completely re-worked because of a false assumption. The account director recognized that tiredness and stress were wasting more hours than the extra time was delivering. At four o'clock in the afternoon, he took the bold step of ordering everyone home with the instruction to wind down, not think about the bid, have a good meal, get some sleep and not to come back before 09.30 the next day. The next day, though not exactly fully recovered, the team worked much better, many problems seemed to have solved themselves (they were just the result of tiredness and stress) and the bid progressed much more smoothly.

SUMMARY

Any manager who has a project disaster on hand needs to be aware that stress has to be kept to a minimum if there is to be a chance of recovering the project. The manager is very likely to be stressed him- or herself and probably too absorbed to notice it easily. The ability to recognize stress in yourself, or just taking the time out to identify being stressed (as opposed to being under pressure) is a necessary step to doing something about it. The self-diagnostic notes in this appendix are here to help in gaining that self-knowledge. Furthermore, being able to diagnose stress in the team and offer some constructive support will also be useful. As a minimum, being calm and making people take breaks can achieve a remarkable amount. However, it is wise to avoid becoming an amateur psychologist as that can easily do more harm than good. If in doubt, involve HR as a first point of call on the way to getting professional advice.

Bibliography

In researching this book, the following books, articles and web sites were helpful and are recommended for further investigation. Please note that they do not represent the complete range of source materials used, nor are they chosen to provide a completely unbiased selection of articles/sites for every topic. Readers are encouraged to use these sources as a starting point for future research of their own. Only by learning from previous disasters is it possible to reduce the chances of experiencing new ones.

BOOKS, REPORTS AND ARTICLES

Adair, John (1988) *Effective time management: How to save time and spend it wisely*, Pan, London

Apollo 13, film, directed by Ron Howard. USA: Universal Pictures, 1995

Armstrong, Michael (2003) *A Handbook of Human Resource Management Practice*, Kogan Page, London

Arroba, Tanya and James, Kim (1987*) Pressure at work: A survival guide*, McGraw-Hill Education, Columbus

Belbin, R Meredith (2003) *Management teams: Why they succeed or fail*, Butterworth Heinemann, Oxford

Butler, Basil (2004) *RAEng/BCS report on IT projects*, Royal Academy of Engineering/British Computer Society, Surrey

Cleland, David I and Kerzner, Harold (1985) *Project Management: Dictionary of Terms*, Van Nost. Reinhold

Comptroller and Auditor General Report, *The Millennium Dome*, (HC 936, Session 1999-2000: 9 November 2000)

Cory, Timothy (2003) *Brainstorming: Techniques for new ideas*, iUniverse.com, New England

De Havilland, Sir Geoffrey (1999) *Sky Fever: The autobiography of Sir Geoffrey De Havilland*, The Crowood Press, Wiltshire

Gleick, James (1988) *CHAOS: Making a New Science*, Sphere Books, London

Godwin, Robert (ed) *Apollo 13: The NASA Mission Reports*, Apogee Books, Texas

Gregory, Anne (ed) (2003) *Public Relations in Practice*, Kogan Page, London

Henslowe, Philip (2003) *Public Relations: A practical guide to the basics*, Kogan Page, London

Jackson, Archie (1998) *Old Pilots, Bold Pilots: Landmarks in commercial aviation – the triumphs and the disasters*, Cirrus Associates, Dorset

Kennedy, Gavin (1997) *Everything is negotiable*, Random House, London

Kharbanda, O P and Pinto, Jeffrey K (1996) *What Made Gertie Gallop? Learning from project failures*, Van Nostrand Reinhold, Sydney

Lovell, Jim and Klugar, Jeffrey (2000) *Apollo 13: Anniversary Edition*, Houghton Mifflin, Massachusetts

Lovell, James A (1975) *Apollo Expeditions to the Moon*, ed. E. M. Cortright, United States Government Printing, Washington, DC

Luft, Joseph (1969) *Of Human Interaction: Johari Model*, Palo Alto, National Press, California

Nickson, David and Siddons, Suzy (1998) *Managing projects*, Butterworth Heinemann, Oxford

Oberg, James (1999) 'Why the Mars probe went off course', *Spectrum Magazine*, December

Oborne, Peter (2004) *Alastair Campbell*, Aurum Press, London

Powell, Ken (1988) *Stress in your life*, Thorsons Publishers, London

Project/programme management survey, *Computer Weekly*, 'The State of IT Project Management in the UK 2002—2003', Report by Chris Sauer and Christine Cuthbertson, Templeton College, University of Oxford Survey sponsored by the French Thornton Partnership

Rich, Jason R (2003) *Brainstorm: Tap into your creativity to generate awesome ideas and tremendous results*, Career Press, New Jersey

Seddon, John (2003) *Freedom from command and control: A better way to make the work, work*, Vanguard Education, Buckingham

Siddons, Suzy (1997) *Delivering training*, CIPD, London

Stewart, Stanley (2002) *Air disasters*, Ian Allen, Surrey

Vroom, Victor H (1964) *Work and Motivation*, John Wiley & Sons, West Sussex

Welch, Jack (2003) *Jack: Straight from the gut*, Headline, London

WEBSITES

An alternative view of the Millennium Dome project; www. millennium-dome.tripod.com/pleasuredome.htm

Bridge disasters; www.iti.northwestern.edu/links/bridges/disasters. html

British Airports Authority — Terminal 5 information; www. baa.co.uk/main/airports/heathrow/terminal_5_frame.html

Channel Tunnel; www.theotherside.co.uk/tm-heritage/background/ tunnel.htm

Expectancy Theory; www.valuebasedmanagement.net/methods _vroom_expectancy_theory.html

GEC information; www.ge.com/en/company/companyinfo/at_a_ glance/hist_leader_info.htm

Holyrood Inquiry web site; www.holyroodinquiry.org/

Hubble Telescope home site; hubble.nasa.gov/servicing-missions/

National Audit Office Report on the Millennium Dome; www. nao.org.uk/pn/9900936.htm

Post-it; www.3m.com/us/office/postit/learn_history_timeline. jhtml

Project management report (survey); www.computerweeklyms.com/ pmsurveyresults

Richard Roger's Millennium Dome; www.greatbuildings.com/ buildings/Millennium_Dome.html

Scaled Composite/Spaceship One website www.scaled.com/

Index